Skillet Cooking
for Camp and Kitchen

Other Cookbooks by A.D. Livingston

Cast-Iron Cooking

Jerky

Sausage

Venison Cookbook

Complete Fish & Game Cookbook

Duck and Goose Cookbook

On the Grill

The Whole Grain Cookbook

Cold-Smoking and Salt-Curing Meat, Fish, & Game

Skillet Cooking
for Camp and Kitchen

More than 101 Modern and Old-Time Recipes for
Jackleg Cooks and Practical Housewives

A. D. Livingston

THE LYONS PRESS
GUILFORD, CONNECTICUT
AN IMPRINT OF THE GLOBE PEQUOT PRESS

Copyright © 2006 by A. D. Livingston

The Lyons Press is an imprint of The Globe Pequot Press

10 9 8 7 6 5 4 3 2 1

Printed in the United States of America

ISBN-13: 978-1-59228-597-6
ISBN-10: 1-59228-597-X

Library of Congress Cataloging-in-Publication data is available on file.

Acknowledgments

A few of the recipes used in this book were adapted from the author's cooking column in *Gray's Sporting Journal*. Acknowledgments to other authors and books are made in the text as appropriate.

Contents

Preface

Frying and sautéing steaks, fish, and other foods in a skillet may seem to be a simple procedure, but there are enough variations and subtleties to make it interesting. It's a hands-on kind of cooking, in which success often depends more on technique, skill, and tender-loving care than on a complicated recipe with a long list of ingredients.

Many of the recipes in this book call for frying or sautéing in a small amount of cooking oil or butter. The reader with a critical eye will note that there is some repetition in these recipes. It's true, I admit, but in self-defense I want to point out that most people don't read a cookbook from one end to the other; indeed, they often look in the index for recipe names and main ingredients to be cooked, then turn only to the pages in play. Thus, I reason, they won't notice a little repetition in this book—and won't be irritated by references from one recipe to another. By comparison, some cookbooks are so full of references that the reader will hopscotch around in the text and may even lose the way back to the starting point.

Being easy and short, most of the recipes in this book can be prepared in camp or on the tailgate, as well as in the home kitchen. Remember, however, that a skillet may not be ideal for everyone. It's a special kind of cooking that requires a close eye: The cook can't merely "set it and forget it." But if you enjoy good eating and take pleasure in your cooking, a skillet is the only pan you need.

—A.D. Livingston

CHAPTER 1

Skilletmanship

Shaking the Skillet, Swirling the Fond, and Savoring the Grimilles, along with Modern Cooking Tips and Old-time Secrets

Any culinary sport seeking advice and illustrations on how to flip pancakes and hash browns into the air and catch them intact and right-side up is reading in the wrong book. Frankly, I don't like to eat off the floor, especially when I have a perfectly good spatula to flip the pancakes and sure-grip tongs to turn the steaks. On the other hand, I suppose, skillet shaking does save some time for those in a hurry, and no doubt makes for a better show on television or behind a short-order bar.

The matter goes a little deeper than mere showmanship, however, and has an influence on the choice of skillet for your personal use. I prefer, for example, to cook in a heavy cast-iron skillet because it heats evenly and cooks good—but unclad cast-iron may be too ugly for some tastes and too heavy for others. Accomplished pan shakers who aspire to showmanship will almost always prefer to have a lighter skillet with a longer, cooler handle. Moreover, some cooks seem to feel a need for expensive or pretty, effeminate utensils in the kitchen. Others don't like to spend less than $100 for a skillet.

Clearly, a brief discussion on skillets in general will get us off to a prudent start, keeping in mind that the proof is usually in the cooking, not in the talking.

What's What

A recently published book on cast-iron skillet cookery had lots of recipes for stove-top Dutch ovens—enough for me to question the honesty of using the word "skillet" in the title. The confusion doesn't stop at the title, either. As I browsed about in the text, a recipe called Skillet-Roasted Clams with Garlic and Parsley caught my eye. Turns out that the clams weren't really roasted in a skillet. The term "roasting" implies cooking with dry heat, usually uncovered in an oven or over an open fire or bed of coals. Instead, the clams in this recipe were actually steamed—and in a Dutch oven, not in a skillet as promised in the name of the recipe. A skillet was not involved in the cooking in any way whatsoever. Moreover, this clam recipe was published in a chapter on outdoor cooking, in which four of the five recipes called for a Dutch oven, not a skillet.

Another book on cast-iron cooking set forth a recipe called Pan-Fried Catfish. In the preamble to the recipe the author says, "In the Southern food lexicon, catfish is nearly always fried, and you certainly need a trusty, seasoned good ol' cast-iron skillet to fry it." Yet, the list of ingredients for the recipe calls for 7 to 9 cups of oil for deep-frying—and the directions clearly say to add the oil to a 4- to 6-quart cast-iron Dutch oven (presumably a stove-top model). No skillet is used in the recipe in any way whatsoever. What the hell is going on?

In any case, I'm not going further into Dutch oven cookery in this book since I feel that most cooks won't confuse a pot with a pan. But here are a few related terms that should perhaps be put into focus before we start cooking.

Skillets and Frying Pans. These interchangeable names apply to shallow metal pans used to fry or sauté meats and other foods. They range in size from 4 inches to about 15 inches across the top of the pan. Since the sides slope down, the bottom will have a smaller diameter. A few models, however, do not slope, being perfectly cylindrical. Although some skillets come with a lid, the cooking is usually done uncovered—or should be. A good deal depends on the size of the skillet and the material from which it was made. These features are discussed under other headings later in this chapter.

Sauté Pans. Similar to skillets, these pans are often made of aluminum, stainless steel, or copper, and a few are made of enameled cast iron. Some have straight sides, but most curve up from the bottom and are a little deeper than a skillet. This curve, together with a long handle, makes the sauté pan much better for fancy skilletmanship such as tossing the food into the air to turn or cool it. Very large sauté pans have a long handle on one side and a D-ring handle on the other. Sauté pans can, of course, be used for panfrying. I might add that some of the illustrations in cookware catalogs show the sauté pan with straight sides and the skillet with curved sides. It's the curve that matters, not the name. Thus, my skillet might well be another cook's sauté pan.

Chicken Fryers. These great pans are deeper than skillets but not as deep as a stove-top Dutch oven. Thus, in function they sort of split the difference between deep-frying and panfrying. They can also be used as a regular skillet, but the high sides sometimes get in the way and make the pan heavier. Most chicken fryers come with a matching lid, which I really can't recommend when using the pan for frying. I like these, used without the lid, for frying enough fish fillets to feed eight to ten people.

Spiders. Although old cast-iron skillets are sometimes called spiders, the real ones have three legs and long handles. These were designed to sit in a bed of coals without mashing them down. Frankly, however, they don't work too well in a campfire, where the ground under the coals is likely to be soft and uneven, in which case a flat skillet balanced on rocks or other support works better (more on campfire cooking at the end of Chapter 12). Spiders are really at their best for use at a fireplace designed for home or cabin cooking, where they can easily be shuffled in and out of a shallow bed of coals spread out on the hearth.

Electric Skillets. These skillets, usually square in shape, plug into standard 120-volt electrical outlets. They usually have a dial temperature control and, in general, work great for frying at medium-high heat. They come with a fitted lid, making them suitable for cooking most one-skillet dishes and for cooking and warming buffet-style foods. Most of these skillets are quite attractive and can be used for serving. I like to have one of these in the kitchen, even if I seldom reach for it.

Griddles. These are flat pans with a shallow lip around the circumference. They work great for some of the skillet recipes in this book, such as blackened fish, but won't work for frying simply because they won't hold enough oil. Round and oval griddles usually have a handle like skillets, but the larger rectangular ones have D-handles on either end. Some of the modern griddles, some pleasingly oval in shape, have a rough, unmachined cooking surface and were intended, I gather, to be used for keeping such foods as fajitas warm while serving. I've never actually seen one of these used for serving, except in an eatery that specialized in fajitas. Fajita pans are nonetheless great for reducing weight and space in camp cookery, and those with a smooth cooking surface do a good job of breakfast bacon and eggs for one or two people.

Skillet Features

Apart from materials and methods of construction, there are several features that vary from one skillet to another. These can have an influence on how the skillet cooks, as well as on how it feels in the hand.

Shape. Square skillets are nice for frying bacon, but for most applications round skillets work best on gas and electric stove burners.

Most skillets have sloping sides, but a few are perfectly round (cylindrical). I prefer the slope. In addition, some skillets and sauté pans don't slope in a straight line from top to bottom, but are rather rounded. These may be better for skillet shakers.

Size. It can be important to match the size of your skillet more or less reasonably with the recipe at hand. An 8-incher will do fine for cooking a couple of ribeyes, but not for making a paella. Size also has a bearing on the ingredients listed in a recipe. When frying, ¼ cup of oil might do just fine with a small skillet, but would barely cover the bottom in a 14-incher.

I have a dozen cast-iron skillets hanging on my kitchen wall, which I find to be a useful arrangement for storing heavy cast-iron pieces. It keeps them aired out, and I think the black pieces on a white wall make an attractive display. The hole in the wall is usually the space where my 8-inch skillet goes. I used it more often during my bachelor days, but when I had several kids in the house and frequently fed them on the fish I caught from the lake, I reached more often for the 12-incher.

I started my marriage, however, with only one skillet—a 10-incher, which was a perfect gift from a wise old friend. I still use it thirty some odd years later, and with great fondness, whereas a dozen Teflons have come and gone, and a few aluminum and steel skillets, mostly gifts for Christmas or Father's Day, clutter the kitchen cabinets.

In any case, the size of the skillet is recommended in some of the recipes in this book. There is some confusion in my mind, however, about exactly how the size is determined. Is the measure across the top or across the bottom? I try to split the difference in my mind, so that half an inch either way won't make much difference.

Skillet Handles. Too often taken for granted, handles can be very important in skillet cookery. Most cooks want a handle that stays cool enough to touch during regular cooking, and long enough to be used with two hands, especially for flipping foods in heavy skillets. Some handles are screwed to the skillet, some are riveted, and some are built in, as in most cast iron. Most of the really good modern skillets have ovenproof handles, but some may not. I've seen imported cast iron with wooden handles, which should not go into a hot oven.

Regular cast-iron skillets all have handles that are rather short, and are pretty much the same size for both large and small skillets. These can get very hot when the skillet is on high heat and must be used with caution. The larger cast-iron pieces, especially the modern ones, have a hand-handle on one side and a D-ring on the other. These are designed for two-handed use when removing a large, hot, heavy skillet from the heat. In general, the cast-iron handles don't work loose and are as durable as the skillet itself, but they are not ideal for putting on a show or for cooking at a campfire on the ground, where a longer handle may be welcome. (See notes on campfire cooking at the end of Chapter 12.) A few small lightweight camp and backpacking skillets have detachable handles. In recent years, manufacturers of expensive cookware have started experimenting with design, and one company offers a hollow stainless-steel handle, saying that it stays cooler than a solid handle.

In any case, I almost always reach for a cast-iron skillet in spite of the limitations of the handle. Suit yourself.

Lids and Pouring Spouts. Most cast-iron skillets have a small pouring spout on either side of the rim. This comes in handy from time to time, but it does complicate the use of a lid. To be effective as a cover, the lid must conform exactly to the spout. Such lids are not standard with most cast-iron skillets with a pouring spout, but they can be purchased on special order, I understand, at a price almost as high as the skillet itself, plus shipping costs. I don't recall actually seeing one of these lids, however, and I don't think I'll ever purchase one for my personal use. I might add that I have had problems with some outdoor Dutch ovens (with three legs and a flanged lid) because the lid didn't fit properly. There may be a problem with tightly fitting lids with any combination made by the sand-casting process. (How cast-iron skillets are made is covered in detail in my book *Cast-Iron Cooking*.)

Some other skillets come with a lid of one kind or another, including glass. These are great if you need a lid, but don't be tempted to use it just because you have it. Some recipes work better without the lid.

Skillet Materials

When choosing a skillet, the modern cook is faced with dozens of choices of materials and combinations thereof, and more miracle choices appear from time to time, often endorsed or promoted by this famous chef or that. Although I studied mechanical engineering in college, with several courses in metallurgy and thermodynamics, I find it hard to make heads or tails of all this. In a recent issue of the Chef's catalog, for example, three or four pages up front pitch a set of rather pricey utensils called All-Clad, with some fifty or sixty skillets and sauté pans available in various sizes and five material combinations, to wit: (1) at the low end of the price range, the regular Stainless Steel is stainless inside and out, with an aluminum inner core; (2) MC has a stainless-steel interior, an aluminum exterior, and a copper core; (3) LTD has a dark anodized exterior, a stainless-steel interior, and an aluminum core; (4) COP-R-CHEF has a thick copper exterior, a core of aluminum, and a stainless-steel interior; and (5) in the COPPER-R-CORE a "stainless steel exterior and cooking surface cloak a core of copper, which provides excellent heat distribution and conductivity between two layers of aluminum." What's a country boy to make of all that?

The quagmire deepens and widens as we go on through the catalog, confronting Emerilware, Anolon, Scanpan, T-FAL, Cuisinart, Le Creuset, and Calphalon One, most of which have three layers of stainless steel, copper, aluminum, or titanium, as well as various ceramic, porcelain, and anodized materials—plus an even more confusing selection of nonstick cooking surfaces, containing such stuff as DuPont's Autograph2 triple-layer coating and Quantanium and "ceramic-titanium." It's hard to know what you need or even what you want, and mistakes can be rather costly.

The choices are usually a little easier in discount stores and in the cookware sections of supermarkets, where you can shake a skillet to see how it fits your hand. Although you might find a simple stainless-steel or aluminum skillet on the shelves of mass-market outlets, most of the choices these days will have some sort of nonstick surface, such as Teflon or some newer miracle clad.

I always try to avoid any skillet with an aluminum cooking surface, partly because I have an old heavy-duty 12-incher that developed pits on the cooking surface and, after storage, shows little spots of white stuff. Stainless steel is a better cooking surface, it seems to me, and is almost nonstick. I would love to have a 7½-inch stainless-steel crêpe pan, which I would feel free to use for frying myself a couple of eggs, whether the French like it or not. But these days it's getting hard to find a simple stainless-steel pan that isn't complicated by multiple layers of aluminum, copper, titanium, and so on—which gets us back to where we started.

Yeah, yeah. I know this text is already tedious, so I'll cut to the end of the materials chase and tell you what I think and feel. I want a 10-inch cast-iron skillet for regular cooking and longevity. (I also like to use 8- and 6-inch skillets for cooking ribeyes.) I also like to have at hand a cheap 8-inch Teflon-coated skillet for cooking a chicken egg or two. As soon as the Teflon starts to peel, I throw the thing away and purchase another at the supermarket. But it's the cast-iron that I reach for when I want such hearty fare as beef-steak, fried chicken, country ham with redeye gravy, and so on. These skillets will last for generations—and some have survived even a house fire.

On the other hand, plain ol' cast-iron skillets don't seem to survive very long or win much shelf space in upscale cookware markets, perhaps because they last too long and don't cost enough for high profit, and maybe because they are heavy and difficult to contain for shipping. We seldom ee cast-iron skillets on television cooking shows—not even on "The Iron Chef"—where the cooks do lots of two-handed pan shaking and aerobatics, and always seem pressed for time and run about the kitchen a lot. Speed may be the key, since cast iron takes longer to heat up and cool down. Weight is also a factor, I'm sure, and advertising dollars may also have a bearing on which skillets are used.

In recent years outlets of expensive cookware have been plugging more and more cast-iron skillets and other cookware coated with some sort of ceramic or porcelain, available in several pastel colors. Pretty, yes, but will they take the heat? I've never used one of these skillets without feeling a little uncomfortable, thermodynamically speaking.

The plain truth is that nothing cooks better than cast iron, nothing lasts longer, and nothing is more affordable. My best advice for a young bull cook is to buy himself a 10-inch plain black cast-iron skillet and learn to keep it rustproof and properly seasoned. Further, I would advise him not to let anyone else touch it. Not even his wife. If this text seems politically incorrect, so be it. As the family grows, he will naturally acquire several more sizes of cast-iron skillets. If he is a lucky man, his bride will eventually learn to appreciate cast iron, or will at least learn not to put it into the mechanical dishwasher.

Sweetening the Skillet

In order to be nonstick, cast-iron skillets must be seasoned properly. In recent years, some of the new skillets come to market preseasoned. These work pretty well, I guess, but I really prefer to season my own. Some of the newer skillets also have a rough cooking surface, whereas I prefer a perfectly slick surface because they produce better gravy. In this regard, an old antique skillet is better than a new one. These can be found in flea markets, junk shops, yard sales, antique shops, and so on.

To season or reseason a cast-iron skillet, scour it out with soap and water, dry it with paper towels, and coat it with lard, suet, or bacon drippings. (Most manufacturers and many books say to use vegetable oil, but I like the animal fat, just like my grandparents used.) Then put the skillet into a 300-degree preheated oven for several hours. (If an oven isn't available, a skillet can also be seasoned on top of the stove or over campfire coals.) When the skillet cools, it will be more or less nonstick—but it will become sweeter and sweeter the longer it is used. Baking cornbread in a cast-iron skillet seems to help the seasoning process.

Once the skillet is sweetened, it should be used and stored properly. After frying fish or chicken, it's best to pour off the grease and wipe the skillet clean with paper towels or a dry rag; do this before the skillet cools, when it will take only a minute. When cooking a steak or chop without much oil, it's best to deglaze the skillet with a little water, maybe with the help of a soft brush—but no soap—and rinse it under running water. Then quickly wipe it dry and put it back onto the stove eye to dry it completely. Finally, coat the inside very lightly with oil and store the skillet in an uncluttered place so it can breathe. I like to keep my 8-incher atop the kitchen range and hang the rest on the kitchen wall.

Note that cooking steaks in a hot skillet without much oil can cause a problem. It's best to deglaze immediately and clean the skillet while it is still hot. The deglazing (see "Deglazing the Skillet," later in this chapter) can be accomplished with wine or stock if you are making a gravy, or you can use plain water if you don't want to keep the fond for the table. Don't throw it out, however, if you have a hungry dog to feed. My dog Nosher claims that the grimilles and fond (as the dredgings and pan liquid are sometimes called and will, I promise, be discussed in more detail a little later) can make gourmet doggie food out of ordinary Gravy Train.

Skillet Cooking Techniques

While the self-made, well-seasoned skillet cook may not need much of the information in this section, I feel that discussion will be helpful just to make sure we are on the same page, if for no other reason. If the novice picks up an idea or two, or if the expert is forced to clarify his thinking a little here and there, so much the better.

Skillet-Fry, Panfry. These synonymous terms refer to frying meats and other foods in a skillet with a little oil. How deep? Personally, I like for the oil to be deep enough to cover about half the thickness of the food. For thin fish fillets, half an inch will do. For chicken breast, a little more will be required. (For safety, however, do not fill the skillet more than half full of oil.) Many of the recipes in this book are cooked by the skillet-fry method. Others are sautéed in a lesser amount of oil, as discussed next.

Sautéing. Steaks and chops cooked in a small amount of oil without any sort of dredging or batter are really sautéed instead of fried. Generally, the sauté works better with very tender cuts of meat that require no beating to enderize them, or with fish fillets. Sautéing can be accomplished on medium heat (often with butter) or on high heat with oils that have a high smoke point, such as peanut oil. There are no hard-and-fast rules, however, and one man's sauté might well be another's fry. The key is in cooking with only a small amount of oil, and without a batter or dusting. The sauté, I might add, leads to superior gravy, as in such dishes as steak au poivre.

Remember also that the sautéing works best with an open skillet. Yes, covering the skillet will help reduce grease spatter going onto the stove, but it will also partly steam the food, tending to producing a soggy surface instead of a crispy one. (But also see the comments under braising, below.)

Deep-Frying. In this popular method of frying, the food is cooked in enough oil to completely cover the food. Usually this will be 3 or 4 inches, but the proper depth is relative. Two inches of oil will deep-fry tiny bay scallop eyes, but not a large chicken breast. More oil is better, within rea-son, because it helps maintain a hot temperature (about 375 degrees Fahrenheit) when the food is added to the fryer. Also, deep-frying is best done without a lid to cover the foods. If covered, the food will be partly steamed, yielding a soft crust instead of the crunch usually associated with fried foods. In any case, this method of cooking is not recommended for skillet cookery. If filled more than half full with oil, a skillet can easily boil over and cause a grease fire. (Tips on fire prevention are found in "Skillet Safety" at the end of this chapter.) The rather deep, skillet-shaped utensils called chicken fryers can sometimes be used for deep-frying, but a deeper pot is better.

Chicken-Fry, Country-Fry. These terms are usually used with beefsteak but can also be applied to venison and other good eats. Essentially, a chicken-fried steak is cut thin, pounded to tenderize it, dusted with flour (or sometimes dipped in egg and rolled in flour), and fried until nicely browned and crisp. It is then topped with a white country gravy, made by pouring most of the cooking oil out of the skillet and then making a gravy with a little flour and some milk. The steaks are plated and the white gravy is poured over them at the table—but only at the last minute. This method combines the flavor of the gravy with the crunch of the steak's crust.

Smother-Fry. This term applies to meats—usually tough cuts—that have been breaded and fried in a skillet. Most of the pan grease is poured off and a thin gravy is made. The meat is then put back into the skillet, covered tightly, and simmered until tender. Sometimes sliced mushrooms and such are also added. The technique is similar to braising, except that the meat is breaded before frying. Smother-frying does not yield a steak or chop with a crunchy crust (as can chicken-frying), but the gravy is usually more flavorful, and more plentiful, and goes nicely with the mashed potatoes or rice.

Braising. This excellent cooking technique is similar to smother-frying except that the food is not dusted with breading or dipped in a batter before being fried. Instead, is it sautéed until browned on all sides, then cooked on low heat in a small amount of liquid, usually water or stock, until it is tender. Braising works best in a skillet with a tight-fitting lid. The food should be stirred and turned from time to time, adding more liquid as needed.

Parboil. Some tough meats are boiled (or, better, simmered) until tender. Then the pieces are breaded and skillet-fried until nicely browned. The technique is often used for cooking tough old squirrels. I seldom apply the technique myself, but my father's parboiled squirrel was memorable. The technique is also used to partly cook some of the tougher foods for a stir-fry or a kabob broil, so that the cooking time in the skillet or wok is equalized for all the ingredients.

Sweating. This term is being used these days to indicate a form of cooking vegetables in a little oil or cooking fat until they are done but not at all browned—the opposite of caramelization. The cooking should be done over rather low heat, and the food is well covered, first with foil and then with a lid to the skillet. I seldom have a need to use this term—or apply the technique without having a name for it. Any time you "sauté" onions until they are translucent but not browned, you are getting pretty close to "sweating," whether you know it or not.

Trying Out. This term refers to a method of melting chunks of animal fat on low heat to render or separate the oil from the tissue. Trying out pork fat, for example, yields lard for cooking purposes and delicious cracklings for noshing, as described in more detail under A Few Cracklings for Old Jack Taylor in Chapter 12. Fat from bear, duck, and some other animals can also be used.

oiling. This term should refer to meats or other foods cooked under a broiler, with the heat coming from the top. The term "pan-broiling" can reasonably be used in skillet cookery, however, especially when one of the raised-ribbed pans is used.

Grilling. This method of cooking is accomplished on a rack or grid over a fire, hot coals, or other heat source. Some meats cooked in a dry skillet or a skillet with a raised-rib bottom are said to be grilled, but not in this book. Many food writers also confuse grilling, which is a quick method of cooking, with barbecuing, which is a long, slow method. The term grill is also applied to a large, flat cooking surface used in short-order restaurants, and, hence, foods cooked on such a heat source are said to be grilled. Because of the confusion, I try to avoid the term (along with the term griddle) in this book.

Roasting. This term means cooking a rather large piece of meat, uncovered, in an oven or over an open fire or coals. It's a dry method of cooking, suitable mostly for tender meats. Tougher cuts are better when cooked by a wet method such as braising. The term has limited use in skillet cookery, but it is used from time to time, as in "roasting chestnuts."

Simmering. In this method of slowly cooking foods, a liquid is often used to tenderize tough meats. Note that simmering does not mean boiling, although small bubbles may break the surface here and there. At sea level, water boils at 212 degrees Fahrenheit; it simmers at about 185 degrees. In some cases, the lowest heat on the kitchen range will be too hot to simmer properly. A flame tamer—usually a flat piece of metal placed between the pan or skillet and the burner—will solve the problem. A skillet can be tightly covered while simmering. If it is left open, more water may have to be added from time to time.

Browning. To cook meat in a skillet on high heat until it is browned all around, usually with the aid of a little cooking oil, is called browning. The cuts of meat can include roasts, steaks, cubes, or burger. With burger, however, the purpose is often to separate the grinds so that the meat doesn't cook in chunks. In this case, the meat is usually cooked to a gray, not to a brown. (See Chapter 3 for more on cooking burger.) So, don't always take the cooking instructions literally.

Searing. Searing means to cook meats briefly on high heat to help seal in the juices. The term is close to browning, but a higher heat is implied. Searing is usually used before longer cooking by some other method and is especially useful when cooking roasts and thick steaks. The term does not often apply to cubed or ground meats.

Caramelize. This culinary term originally applied to sugar that has been heated until it melts and turns lightly brown. These days it is widely used in cookbooks, in magazine articles, and, especially, on television shows to refer to everything from burnt onions to seared steaks. I suppose the term is useful, but I hold suspect any word that ends in -ize. The old term "brown" used as a verb as in the directive "brown the onions" is a shorter word and a better one.

Skillet in the Oven. Although used primarily on top of the heat, a skillet also makes a good pan for cooking in an oven. A cast-iron skillet is especially useful for this since it has an ovenproof handle. Many people consider a cast-iron pan the very best for baking cornbread, and even biscuits. When cooking thin fish fillets, I sometimes sauté them on top of the stove and then put them under a preheated broiler to brown the top, all without turning the tender fillet even once. I do, however, want to point out that "oven-frying" is one of the more absurd terms in culinary lingo. You have to use oil to fry anything.

Skillet Cooking Tools and Practical Tips

In addition to the important methods of cooking, such as frying and sautéing, the compleat skillet chef will also master a few more subtle techniques, cooking tools and aids, and culinary tricks. Here's a brief commentary.

Wooden Spoons. These should be required tools for stirring anything in a metal skillet, pot, or pan, nonstick or otherwise. They don't make as much noise as metal spoons, and they don't constantly scrape or dent the surface of the pan. I might add that some professional chefs on TV don't always reach for wooden spoons, clanking away, metal to metal, raising goose bumps on sensitive guests and viewers.

In some cases, as when making a dark roux, wooden spoons don't get as hot as a metal spoon during long, slow stirring. For deglazing the pan, however, wooden spoons are not quite right for scraping up all the bottom edgings for the gravy. In this case, a wooden spatula might be in order, and even a metal spatula carefully wielded will do a good job, as discussed below.

Spatulas. A spatula is often a handy skillet tool, and sometimes two are better then one, as when turning tender fish fillets during the sauté. Always, a thin spring-steel spatula with a handle of normal length works better than a thick one with a long handle. Some of the cheap metal spatulas with thick blades will tear up a burger while you try to get under it, and long ones billed for outdoor grilling are awkward to use, especially with a skillet with high sides.

In addition to turning burgers, eggs, and so on, I also use a spatula for helping to deglaze the skillet. They scrape up the bottom dredgings (grimilles) better than a rounded spoon. See also "Deglazing the Skillet", below.

A good many cooks, including some short-order sharps who work on a flat grill, use a spatula to press down on burgers and other foods during cooking, squeezing out the good juice. I am guilty of this sin from time to time, usually when I'm in a hurry or have a nervous need to do something while the burger cooks, but I don't recommend the practice.

Nor do I recommend flipping pancakes or eggs or burgers into the air in order to turn them, but boys will be boys. If you are so inclined, get a wide spatula. Most of the wide ones have slots or holes in the middle to drain out the grease. The long, narrow ones are usually solid and are not as easy to use as a regular blade, especially in skillet cookery. They work a little better on a large griddle or a cookie sheet.

Deglazing the Skillet. A lot of cooks use this technique without knowing that it has a fancy name in culinary lingo. If questioned, they would mumble something about scraping up the browned bits from the bottom of the skillet. This is best accomplished shortly after pouring a little wine or stock into the hot skillet and at once stirring and scraping the bottom, preferably with a wooden spoon or, even better, with a wooden spatula. After deglazing, a sauce, gravy, or stock is made by one means or another, always using the bottom dredgings for flavor.

The browned bits and pieces are called fond in some circles, a term that also applies more properly to a stock made by deglazing, as in fond brun or fond blanc. In rural Louisiana, the bits and pieces are sometimes called grimilles. These are a conscious contribution to some good cooks' recipes and technique, and they are especially important in a skillet gravy or sauce made after cooking meats on rather high heat without much oil.

Deglazing a skillet with a little water immediately after cooking a steak or chop also helps with the cleanup. More practical uses of deglazing are set forth in some recipes throughout the book, and especially in the gravy chapter.

Shaking the Skillet. A lot of chefs and jackleg cooks like to shake the pan a time or two while cooking diced meats and vegetables. The motion is simply a quick back-and-forth shuffle, often without taking the skillet off the heat. The idea, other than giving the cook something to do, is to keep the food from sticking or from scorching on the bottom. Sometimes the skillet is lifted off the heat to help cool things down during the shaking. Other sharps use the skillet shake when cooking gravy and sauces with the aid of oil and flour of some sort, saying it "brings the sauce together" and keeps the gravy from "separating."

Generally, a heavy cast-iron skillet doesn't shake quite as nicely as one of steel or aluminum. But they don't need to be shaken as often, I submit. Also, a long-handled skillet works a little better, especially for a two-hands shake.

Note that merely shaking the skillet doesn't necessarily turn the contents over. This bit of showmanship requires a quick shuttle-and-flip motion, as discussed below.

The Swirl. This nifty motion, accomplished with the wrist, swishes the contents around, as when melting butter.

Tongs. These come in handy for turning and handling hot steaks, chicken pieces, and so on. They aren't stuck into the meat like forks, thereby helping hold in all the good juices. Those tongs with rather short handles are easier to work and give a better grip, making it less likely to drop a chicken breast into hot grease. The better tongs are spring-loaded, meaning that they open on their own, making them easier to use. The business ends can have several shapes. One kind has a claw-like grip with three toes. These are all right, but my favorite tongs have scalloped ends.

Flipping. A number of chefs like to flip the contents of a skillet into the air, sometimes turning it with the same motion. The technique is not eded for eggs or flapjacks, which are better turned with the aid of a good spatula, but it does come in handy for stirring and turning chunks of vegetables or perhaps meats, as when making hash browns from finely diced potatoes. Flipping works best with a light skillet with a deeply curved bottom and a long handle. Large skillets should have a long handle for two-handed use. I won't try to describe the motion used to toss the food into the air, ostensibly turning it over, but it involves a shuffle and an upward lift or flip.

Watch a few television shows if you want to observe the technique in action. "The Iron Chef" or "Emeril Lasagna" would be good place to start. It doesn't seem to matter to the TV chefs if some of the food falls onto the stove or onto the floor. They don't even slow down to clean up the mess. If left on the floor in a busy restaurant, however, spilt food would be quite slippery. It would also cause the customer's serving to be a little short. Maybe that's where the term "short-order cook" came from. But I don't recommend that the food be picked up off the floor and added back to the skillet.

All joking aside, a lot of people enjoy flipping the food into the air, and I'll be quick to say that I enjoy watching a good chef do his thing. But I'm not good at it, and I don't want to trade my heavy cast-iron pieces for lightweight aluminum and stainless steel. If you do want to experiment with flipping, be sure to stick with dishes that don't contain much hot oil.

Tilting. The experienced cook will sometimes tilt a skillet to concentrate the oil or pan liquid to one side in order to increase its depth. The technique comes in especially handy for frying small pieces of meat for a skillet stir-fry. Some TV chefs seem tilt the skillet in order to spill out some liquid to cause a fire, as discussed under flaming.

Tapping. I have seen Oriental chefs tilt a large skillet to corner the contents, then, holding the tilt, start tapping the bottom of the skillet rhythmically with a chopstick. I don't know why, but I assume that this somehow helps the texture of whatever is being cooked—surely something airy and delicate and soufflé-ish. In any case, I don't see why the round end of a wooden spoon wouldn't be just as good for tapping.

Flaming. Called flambé in highfalutin' circles, this old method of finishing off a dish with a dramatic flare consists of adding a little brandy or other ardent spirit at the end of the preparation and then setting it ablaze, hopefully in view of the diners. Some chefs can accomplish this by tilting the skillet or otherwise spilling or splashing a little of the liquor onto the burner, but some us who are more careful or less skilled set the fire with a long match or some sort of lighter. In any case, the method fits in nicely with skillet cookery, partly because the showman, with only a good pot holder, can easily bring the flaming food directly to the serving table. I have used the method from time to time throughout my culinary life, but not often. Usually when drinking or courting, or both. Some of my guests would recognize me as being a rank amateur at the flambé—and others might be frightened by the showmanship.

A Level Cooking Surface. Frying with a small amount of oil is best accomplished in a level skillet. Otherwise, one side of the skillet might be dry while the other side contained more oil than needed. With electric stoves there can be a little variation between one cooking eye and another, but the big problem, if one exists, is usually an improperly installed stove or a sagging floor. The tilt can be adjusted by screw-in feet at each corner of the stove, where it sits on the floor. Usually an adjustable wrench is the only tool required to level the stove, used along with an ordinary carpenter's level. If you don't have a level at hand, use the skillet itself with just enough oil in it to cover the bottom. If the oil flows to one side, you have a problem. Gas ranges can also be out of level and can be trued by the same method.

Needless to say, deep-frying in a skillet should also be done on a level eye or burner. Otherwise, the oil would be more likely to boil over or slosh out and start a grease fire.

In campfire cooking a perfectly level surface is often hard to achieve, but a little care before heating the skillet can help. If cooking on a rack, it should be leveled before heating the skillet. When resting the skillet on rocks or logs, it often helps to level the skillet with your hand from time to time while cooking, or perhaps tilt it the other way to even things out.

Bacon Press. These metal cooking aids, some shaped like a trivet with a handle or an old hand iron, are designed to sit on bacon to keep it from curling up while cooking. They work, but they take the characteristic wave out of bacon. The compleat skillet cook will own one of these, although he may not always be able to find it. I always get mine ready for cooking sliced hog jowl (which curls even worse than bacon) to go along with my New Year's Hoppin' John and, sometimes, to tame a wayward fish fillet.

atter Screens. Those chefs who feel a need to prevent the spatter of hot oil during the fry should consider using spatter screens instead of skillet covers. The covers trap the steam and tend to make a soft crust instead of a crunch. Spatter screens are available in several sizes from retail outlets that traffic in kitchenware.

Slotted Spoons and Skimmers. Slotted spoons help drain the oil from fried foods as they are removed from the skillet. A wire skimmer, often used in wok cookery, is even better. Wire baskets are used for deep-frying. These are suitable for draining fried foods, but in too many cases the top pieces simply drip oil onto the bottom.

Brown Bags. Many writers will specify absorbent paper for draining fried foods. This would include paper towels, but the old-style brown paper grocery bags are better. I even use them for serving fried foods at informal gatherings, especially when eating from an outdoor table. Sometimes I'll put the whole bag onto a large platter, metal tray, or baking sheet. It is important not to pile the fried foods onto the bags, in which case the top pieces would simply drip onto the bottom ones. A single layer works best for draining fried foods, using more than one bag, if need be. The food can be piled after draining, if more space is needed.

Breading

Most fried foods are first coated with flour or meal, either dry (dredging) or in a thick liquid batter. I lean heavily toward a dredging for skillet cooking. A thick batter works better with deep-frying.

Dredging. Many cooks simply dust skillet-bound steaks, fish, and other meats with all-purpose wheat flour before frying, but some culinary sports use several kinds of flour or meals as well as dry bread crumbs to dredge the meat. The Japanese panko, for example, makes a crunchy crust if used correctly, and traditional Jewish cookery makes use of matzo meal (made from the unleavened matzo bread) for frying. In parts of Africa, ground black-eyed peas are used for dusting meats to be fried—and for making what I believe to be the original hush puppy. Personally, I am fond of using stone-ground white cornmeal as a dusting, especially for frying the perfect fish, although I know that blue cornmeal is quite the rage in some quarters at the moment. Note that yellow cornmeal, as compared to white, makes a harder coating and tends to come off during cooking. White meal (if made from whole-kernel corn) is not as gritty, sticks better, and has more flavor, as I have argued before.

Wild foods enthusiasts should know that many seeds and nuts, such as mesquite beans and sunflower seeds, can be ground and used as a dredging for frying. Many Southerners will be quite surprised to learn that the kuzu flour they purchased at high prices from Asian markets really is made from the kudzu, a high-climbing vine plant that has gone wild in some states. The leaves and stems of kudzu are edible and easy to pick, but it's the huge roots that are prized in Japan for making a starch to thicken soups as well as to dredge foods to be fried. You can buy prepared kuzu in some specialized Asian markets—but do-it-yourselfers should be warned that digging kudzu is not an easy task. The bulbs can weigh up to 700 pounds.

Of course, many cooks will want to mix flour, cornmeal, and so on, making their own secret recipe. Also, many recipes call for dusting the meat with flour, then dunking it in milk, buttermilk, or lightly beaten chicken egg, and finally rolling it in cornmeal, bread crumbs, or even something like sesame seeds. This will make a thicker coating with more crunch. But the combinations are endless.

I usually prefer to dust the meat or fish sparsely with a fine meal or flour, or to shake it in a brown bag, without the use of chicken egg or other goo to make it stick. (If the egg is omitted, however, the coating tends to come off during cooking.) Many cooks prefer to pour a little flour on a flat surface, or a plate, and flip-flop the meat or other food in it, then shake off the excess.

There are many variations on this technique, including the Batter Pro, a gadget sold on TV. With this gadget you put the flour into a bottom container, add a strainer, and top with another container. The meat is shaken, then the whole thing is turned over. The meat stays on top and the flour shakes to the bottom, ready for another shake. The Batter Pro looks great for anyone who does lots of frying and wants to dust chicken or fish—but it is misnamed. A dusting is not a batter.

Battering. Using a batter instead of a dry coating calls for dipping the food in a thick but liquid mixture of sifted flour, water or milk, and egg. Again, the variations are endless. The Japanese are proud of their tempura, and the Koreans like to use a batter made with buckwheat flour, hich is especially sticky and holds fritters together nicely. Personally, I usually avoid batters when I cook, partly because they are messy and because they tend to sog up lots of grease. On the plus side, properly made batters can produce a delicate, airy crunch, and batter-fried foods are perfect for soaking up lots of dipping sauce such as the Vietnamese nuoc cham (see recipe in Chapter 6). In any case, the batter route works best with deep-frying in a pot instead of in a skillet. Contact with the bottom of a skillet tends to deflate the fritter.

Skillet Oils

Let's face it: Cooking oil is a very important part of skilletmanship, especially for frying and sautéing. The modern cook has a wide variety from which to choose. The choice is often based on regional preference and the cook's upbringing, and, in recent years, has been highly influenced by such medical topics as cholesterol.

Measuring oil for skillet cookery recipes can be a little tricky and very misleading. If a recipe calls for ¼ cup of oil, for example, it might work just fine for an 8-inch skillet but would be too thin for a 14-incher. For regular skillet-frying, it's always best to measure the oil in terms of depth in the skillet, usually about an inch or less. Of course, you simply pour in an estimated depth and don't have to dip a ruler into the skillet.

It's always a mistake to put too much oil in a skillet, or to overcrowd the skillet with chicken or other foods to be fried, thereby raising the height of the oil. Hot oil is dangerous, accounting for countless burns and many home fires. I'll have more on this topic later in this chapter. Meanwhile, here's my take on a few kinds of oil suitable for skillet cookery.

Peanut Oil. Having a high smoke point and a mild flavor, peanut oil is excellent for frying. It doesn't readily absorb flavors, making it a good choice for those of us who reuse oil from the deep fryer. (Strain it through a coffee filter and store it in a cool, dark place.) I have used more peanut oil than any other kind, no doubt because I was born and raised on a peanut farm, where we grew a hundred or more tons of peanuts a year. (Cooks from the Corn Belt may have their own obvious favorite!) In recent years, however, peanut oil has become increasingly expensive, as compared to corn and canola oil.

Note that my comments here apply to peanut oil made in this country. Peanut oil from China, I understand, may have a stronger flavor.

Corn Oil. Very popular in the United States, corn oil is rather tasteless and has a high smoke point, making it a good choice for frying. Corn oil is inexpensive and is widely used.

Canola Oil. This is a marketing-inspired new name for the old rapeseed oil. The term originated in Canada, where it is the most widely used cooking oil and where it was also known as "lear oil," standing for low-erucic-acid rapeseed. Under whatever name, canola oil is suitable for frying. It has become increasingly popular in the United States because of its good properties healthwise, being lower in saturated fat than most any other oil—only 6 percent as compared to 18 percent for peanut oil and 79 percent for palm oil. What's more, canola oil is bland and inexpensive.

Sesame Oil. An excellent cooking oil, having a high smoke point (about 420 degrees Fahrenheit), sesame oil is now available in most supermarkets. It should not be confused, however, with the stronger and darker Asian toasted sesame oil that is used as a flavoring in stir-fries and similar dishes. The seasoning type of sesame oil is usually sold in the Chinese or ethnic section of the supermarket and is a good deal more expensive.

Olive Oil. Much the rage these days in San Francisco and some other urban centers, olive oil can be used for either frying or sautéing. It's not my favorite from a purely culinary viewpoint (except for a salad dressing), but I, like many other people, use it often because it is said to be good for one's health. Several grades are available, and critics have developed a vocabulary for describing the tastes. For sautéing, I usually use an extra-virgin oil from the same bottle that I use for the salad dressing. In general, most olive oil is a little too expensive to be widely used for deep-frying, but don't rule it out if you are sold on its health-giving qualities. Shop around, maybe looking in Sam's or some such wholesale club. Olive oil is cheaper by the gallon and may be competitive even with peanut oil, if you can buy it locally without added shipping costs.

Vegetable Oil. Popular and inexpensive, this is probably the best-seller in modern cooking oils, partly because the name suggests that it is a healthy product. It is usually a combination of oils from vegetable matter and can include oils from corn, canola, soybean, cottonseed, sunflower seeds, and so on. Be sure, however, that it does not contain a high proportion of expensive ls such as peanut or olive. If in doubt, check the contents as listed on the label. The more important oils are listed first, by volume.

Of course, any cooking oil expressed from vegetable matter, seeds, or nuts is vegetable, including the ones discussed above along with a variety of lesser-known products such as grapeseed oil, hazelnut oil, pumpkinseed oil, and so on.

Vegetable Shortening. This is a soft but solid form of cooking oil made by chemically transforming the properties by hydrogenation. In recent years it has acquired a bad name among health food freaks, and I get the impression that it is used more often in bakery than in skillet cookery. Healthy properties aside, it does, however, make a good skillet oil and is a favorite of many chefs. When listed in the contents of printed recipes, it is often called Crisco, the most popular brand.

The term shortening in general can apply also to animal fats that form a soft shortening when cooled.

Butter and Margarine. Butter is a favorite medium for frying eggs, brook trout, and other foods. It burns easily, however, and must be watched carefully during the cooking. In order to increase the smoke point, some jacklegs mix butter and beef suet for panfrying. Clarified butter and ghee work better for frying simply because they have some of the milk solids removed. These can be purchased in some markets, or you can make your own as discussed further in Chapter 12.

At one time during my culinary career, margarine was deemed safer to eat than butter; consequently, thousands of old recipes were rewritten with margarine in the list of ingredients. In more recent years, however, margarine got a bad name in the health food business—and now a lot of chefs have gone back to butter. I prefer butter—and salted butter lasts longer and tastes better than unsalted. But some editors for books and magazines have an urge to change all butter to unsalted these days whether the author likes it or not.

Animal Fat. Not too long ago in our culinary history, most of our cooking oil was derived from animal fat, including lard (from pork) and suet (from beef). The demand for oil influenced the way we raised and fattened our livestock. More fat was better. This trend is best illustrated by the breeding and development of the fat-tailed sheep in the Middle East, once illustrated with a sheep hauling its enormous tail around in a little wagon. The modern trend, however, is to develop pigs and beef without much fat and to encourage the use of "range" animals instead of those fattened in a feed lot. In addition to domestic livestock, some wild animals, such as bear, produce a good cooking fat.

Although excellent for frying and sautéing, lard and suet are becoming increasingly hard to find in supermarkets. You can purchase pork and beef fat and render your own. If you enjoy the old ways of doing things and yearn for some good skinless cracklings, see Chapter 12 for more details.

I still enjoy cooking with lard and suet from time to time, but I will admit that modern thinking on animal fat's contribution to heart problems for Homo sapiens has led me to lean more and more toward vegetable oil. If the charges turn out to be unfounded, I'll be mad as hell.

Skillet Safety

Hot skillet handles, popping grease, and accidental contact with the rim of the skillet cause many minor burns—but grease fires are the biggest hazard. Here are some talking points to help minimize the danger. Ignore them at your peril.

Oil Level. Never fill a skillet more than half full of cooking oil, and never overcrowd a skillet with fish, chicken, or other foods to be fried. Pictures in magazines and on television shows often err in this direction. A full skillet not only contains more oil to burn, but is also more likely to boil over and catch fire from the stove burner, especially when using gas heat.

Temperature and Smoke. Always stay alert for smoke and adjust the temperature of your skillet accordingly. You can see the smoke and you can smell it, and usually you can sense when a skillet is too hot simply by the sizzle it makes. If you are smart, you'll have a modern smoke detector in working order in the kitchen. Yeah, yeah. I know. Smoke detectors can be a pain in the neck, as they often sound off long before you think there is danger of an outright fire, but, even so, they are a good reminder that you need to watch your skillet closely.

Extinguishing a Grease Fire. Once the oil in a skillet catches on fire, smoke will quickly ruin the paint job in a kitchen and possibly in the rest of the house. The impulse of most cooks will be to grab the skillet handle and rush for the back door to get the fire out of the house. Sometimes the handle is too hot to hold onto, or the fire licks back onto the hands, causing the skillet and burning oil to be dropped on the floor, causing a larger fire or burning the cook, or both. Sometimes opening the back door with one hand while trying to hold the burning skillet with the other will cause an incoming draft of air, causing the fire to sweep back onto the cook's hand and face.

Some people keep a small fire extinguisher in the kitchen, which of course is a very good idea. Just be sure that it will handle a grease or oil fire. My personal choice—which I have exercised more than once—is to keep a box of baking soda handy. When sprinkled into the hot skillet, the soda will cause a gas that quickly extinguishes the fire. I always keep a box of soda within easy reach of the kitchen stove, and it's hell to pay for anyone who hides it in a cabinet.

Some other people say to cover a burning skillet with a lid, which is, I suppose, better than making a run for the door, but I have never had to do this. Most cast-iron skillets are hard to cover tightly because of the pouring spout on either side.

One of the worst things you can do to a skillet fire is to pour water into it. Oil and water don't mix and will cause an even more dangerous fire. Since skillet fires are so common, I would suggest holding a family fire drill on this matter, emphasizing the use of the fire extinguisher or the box of soda, or both.

Camp cooks don't have to worry about the kitchen paint when the skillet catches on fire. The best bet is to let it burn. That way, all you'll lose is a little oil and a few fish or whatever you were frying.

Pot Holders, Mittens, and Cooking Gloves. Every Christmas I get two or three sets of pot holders, some lovingly hand-sewn and some made in the shape of a mitten. Yet, I can seldom find one when I need it quickly! Often I'll make do with a dry—never wet—dishcloth or towel. (Wet cloth will quickly cause hot steam, which will burn you or cause you to drop the skillet, or both.) What I really want for cast iron, however, is a pair of cooking gloves. These give a sure grip and are designed to withstand some heat—and the handle of a cast-iron skillet gets very, very hot. There are several of these on the market, and I like to think of them as being made of "asbestos," but most of them are probably some sort of leather and cloth combination. I also have a set of rubberized cooking gloves that came with my old Showtime Rotisserie, but I usually save these for use when shucking oysters, where the waterproof feature is needed. Bottom line: Get yourself a good set of cooking gloves and have them at hand before you start cooking with cast-iron skillets. Many of the other skillets have a longer and cooler handle.

Trivet. A short-legged or otherwise raised stand is handy for holding hot skillets and pots, thereby keeping them off the surface of the table or countertop. Having a trivet at ready will not only protect the table or countertop but will also permit the cook to get rid of a hot pan in a hurry, making it a safety device.

Frying Explosive Foods. Some foods can pop violently when cooking in hot oil, sometimes resulting in painful burns on the cook's hands and arms, and even the face of one who likes to hunker down over the skillet. Chicken livers and fish roe are especially prone to pop. A lady friend of mine advised me to wrap mullet roe in aluminum foil before trying it. Well, it stopped the spattering all right, but the roe was more steamed than fried. Some people will want to cover the skillet to contain the spatter, but that too alters the frying process. My best advice is to fry as usual—but be careful, stand back, and use long tongs to turn the chicken livers.

Treating Grease Burns. I hesitate to give medical advice on this matter, partly because the popular remedies for grease burns, like those for snakebite, seem to change every time I read up on the subject. My best advice is to run clean cold water over the burn as soon as possible to cool it down. Ice helps, but a steady stream of cold water is better. If the burn is at all serious, see a doctor as soon as you can. Secondary infection is a big problem with burns, and these can set in days after the accident.

Years ago, when I lived out in the country, I caught myself on fire at two o'clock in the morning, while cooking a very late supper. While holding a book open in my right hand, I put a skillet on the rear eye of the stove—but I turned on the front burner by mistake. Then I leaned against the stove to continue reading, and, before I knew it, my shirt was on fire. I ran up through the house, tearing off the shirt (a synthetic thing) and a cotton T-shirt, planning to roll myself in a quilt on the foot of the bed to smother the flame. Fortunately, I got the shirt off without having to use the quilt, but in the process I burned my right hand in addition to my back. I washed down with cold water and immediately drove my car—an old Volkswagen with stick shift—to the emergency room of a small hospital about 20 miles away, sitting up straight to keep my back off the seat and working the gear with my burned right hand while steering with my left. The burns hurt pretty bad before I got treatment, but I think I did the right thing. These days I would probably call 911 instead of trying to drive myself.

Clearly, a skillet can be a dangerous utensil—and cooking with one on high heat is a full-time job. Never leave the skillet handle sticking over the edge of the stove, especially if you have small children on the floor or good ol' boys wrestling in the kitchen.

CHAPTER 2

Beef and Pork in the Skillet

**Steaks Cognac à la Joe Dogs Iannuzzi,
Bornean Pig Chops, A.D.'s Un-Lucullan Ribeye,
Veal Parmigiana, and Other Choice Eats**

For the most part, really good steaks and chops
are ideal for cooking in the skillet. Tougher cuts can also be
used, sometimes following a Plan B approach in case Plan A
doesn't pan out just right, and these less-expensive meats
can be even more rewarding to the jackleg cook. This chapter
deals mostly with thin cuts of beef and pork. Ground meats
are covered separately in Chapter 3. Also, some of the
recipes in the game chapter (Chapter 5) can easily be used
to cook beef and pork. Best of all, I hope the recipes and

methods set forth in the chapter on gravy (Chapter 11) will inspire more people to try the old ways, with a skillet in one hand and a wooden spoon in the other.

Some of the recipes below illustrate the terms "chicken-fried," "smother-fried," and so on in more detail than we set forth in Chapter 1, and the techniques can be used with other recipes. Learn the best way to cook a chicken-fried steak, for example, and the lesson can easily be adapted for venison chops in camp cookery. That's the great attraction to skillet cookery, so that every jackleg can easily add a pinch or two of his own secret ingredient without changing the results too drastically. In short, properly prepared chicken-fried steak is good with or without a little chopped parsley in the gravy. So, let's start with this old favorite of Mid-America.

Chicken-Fried Steaks

These are tender steaks, often beaten or cubed, that are dredged and fried with a crispy outside. Then they are topped with a skillet gravy, often a white one. Beef steaks from chuck, cut from ⅜ to ½ inch and duly beaten, are best for this recipe.

beef chuck steaks (about a pound)
peanut oil
all-purpose flour
milk (at room temperature)
water
chicken egg
salt and freshly ground black pepper

Sprinkle the steak on both sides with salt, pepper, and a little flour, then beat it with the edge of a heavy plate or saucer. Turn and repeat several times until the meat is quite tender. Lightly whisk the egg and a little milk. Dust the steaks with flour, dip in the egg mixture, let the excess drip off, and then dredge in flour. Shake off the excess flour and set the steaks aside while you heat about half an inch of peanut oil in a skillet.

Fry the steaks for 2 or 3 minutes on each side until golden brown and a little crispy, turning once. Remove the steaks to a heated serving platter but do not cover.

Pour off most of the skillet oil, saving about 2 tablespoons. Slowly add 2 tablespoons flour, stirring with a wooden spoon. Stir in about 1 tablespoon of water and reduce the heat. Slowly stir in 1 cup of milk, or a little more depending on how thin you want the gravy. Cook and stir for a few minutes, shaking the skillet as you go, until you have a nice white gravy.

Pour the gravy over the steaks (or into a gravy boat) and serve hot, along with mashed potatoes and vegetables of your choice. It is important to hold the gravy until the last minute. That way, you'll have a rare treat of a crunchy steak in a flavorful gravy.

Smother-Fried Steaks

Here's a method for cooking very tough steaks, perhaps from an animal of maturity and character, as they like to say in Texas. It's a great recipe for camp cooking, if you have the patience and the skill to simmer the steak in the gravy long enough without burning it. In a sense, it is the exact opposite to Chicken-Fried Steaks, which just goes to show you that there's more than one trick in the skillet cook's bag. Note that the previous recipe works best with comparatively tender cuts of meat; this one, with tough cuts. The Chicken-Fried Steaks recipe offers a certain crunch with the gravy; this one, however, makes the best possible gravy. (For more on gravy, see Chapter 11.)

tough steaks
chopped onion
chopped fresh mushrooms
flour
cooking oil
salt and freshly ground black pepper
water

Dust the steaks with flour, salt, and pepper. Beat each steak on one side, then turn and beat the other. Sprinkle with flour and beat again. Heat a little oil in a skillet, getting it hot enough to spit back at you. Give the steaks a final dusting with flour and quickly fry for 2 or 3 minutes on each side, turning once, then remove from skillet. Cook in several batches, if necessary.

Pour off most of the cooking oil, keeping about 1 tablespoon. Sauté the onion and mushrooms until the pieces start to brown around the edges. Add a little water to deglaze the skillet, scraping up any grimilles that have stuck to the bottom of the pan. Make a paste with flour and water, then slowly pour it in, stirring, until you have a thin gravy. Bring to a light boil, then put the steaks back into the skillet. Lower the heat, cover tightly, and simmer for 2 hours or longer, until the steaks are fork tender. Stir from time to time and add more water as needed. (If you don't have a tightly fitting lid, use whatever you can rig; then stir and add water more often.)

Serve hot with rice or mashed potatoes, along with green beans and other vegetables or salad and maybe some chewy French bread to help sop up some of that wonderful skillet gravy.

Steaks Cognac à la Joe Dogs Iannuzzi

Here's a recipe cooked by Joseph "Joe Dogs" Iannuzzi at a safe house in Florida, where he was awaiting important news concerning his fate. In his *Mafia Cookbook,* Joe Dogs said he wanted to serve something special, just in case it would be his last supper. The recipe calls for four filets mignons of about 8 ounces each. Since I have trouble finding these in my neck of the woods, and don't have Mafia money to order them via airmail delivery, I usually cook the dish with four regular ribeyes cut 1½ inches thick.

4 tender steaks of about 8 ounces each

8 rather large mushrooms, sliced

2 medium to large onions, chopped

½ cup beef stock

½ cup very good cognac

3 tablespoons extra virgin olive oil

salt and freshly ground black pepper to taste

Heat the olive oil in a 12 inch skillet and cook the steaks, turning once, until they are done to your liking. (Medium rare for me.) Stack the steaks on a heated platter and set aside.

Add a little more olive oil to the skillet if needed. Quickly sauté the onions and mushrooms for about 8 minutes, stirring several times. Add the beef stock, cognac, salt, and black pepper. Flame the skillet to burn off the alcohol. Then simmer until the liquid is reduced by half. Put the steaks back into the sauce and reheat, turning once.

Serve with a baked potato and vegetables of your choice. Joe Dogs recommends his Asparagus Hollandaise, but I'll settle for simply steamed asparagus, cooked only a short time to retain a slight crunch. Of course, a good red wine and a chewy Italian bread go nicely with the dish.

Note: A number of other recipes for skillet steaks are also good, such as steak au poivre and Steak Diane. I can't cover all these here, but I would like to call attention to an old recipe for cooking in a dry skillet and to a recipe I like to use for cooking for myself in a 6-inch cast-iron skillet, both covered below.

Dry Salt Steak

This unusual method of cooking steak seems to seal in the juices better than other methods, and the results are not as salty as one might think. A popular family cookbook directs the reader to wash the cooked steak before serving. Don't do it! I normally use ribeyes or chuckeyes about 1½ inches thick for this technique. Any good steak will do, but those with lots of marbling work best.

Note that this method does make some smoke. If you don't have a good vent over your kitchen stove, it may be best to save this method of cooking for the patio. It's also a very good camp recipe, thanks partly to the Spartan list of ingredients. I normally use a sea salt for this recipe, but regular table salt works just fine. Avoid very coarse salt, however.

good beef steak
sea salt (regular grind)

Sprinkle a thin coat of salt onto the skillet, almost covering the bottom. Heat the skillet until it is very hot. Dry the steak with a paper towel and lay it onto the salt. Sear without turning for 4 minutes. Turn and cook the other side for 4 minutes. It should be crispy brown on the outside and rosy moist inside. Serve hot, along with potatoes, salad, and whatever you like with your steak.

A.D.'s Un-Lucullan Ribeye

Not having as many servants as Lucullus, the Roman epicure who insisted on a full table even when dining alone, I confess to cutting back a little when cooking a steak for myself only. I think it's best to drink the brandy after dinner instead of burning it in some showy recipe like Steak Diane, which I would be more likely to cook for a lady love. Often, I admit, I do not bother to deglaze the skillet, forfeiting the fond in favor of a low-fat meal. I do, however, cook the steak rare or medium rare and cut it immediately on the plate, letting some good red juice run out to flavor the carbohydrates. (Most recipe writers will advise you to let the steak rest a little before serving so that more of the juices will stay inside. This may be something to consider if you have guests likely to go squeamish—suit yourself.) I cook a boneless ribeye in a 5-inch cast-iron skillet, into which it fits snugly, browning the ends as well as top and bottom. A bone-in ribeye or T-bone won't fit in a small round skillet snugly.

1 ribeye steak about 1½ inches thick
soy sauce
black pepper
salt as needed
olive oil

Grind some black pepper onto each side of the steak, pressing it into the meat with your fingertips. Put the steak into a small container and pour a little soy sauce over it. Let it sit at room temperature for an hour or so while you get the potatoes, salad, bread, and so on ready. (If longer, put the container into the refrigerator.)

Drain the soy sauce off the steak and discard (unless you opt for gravy). Heat the skillet on high until it spits back at you. Add a little olive oil to the skillet. When the oil starts to smoke, put the steak in with your tongs, centering it nicely. Set your timer for 3 minutes. Do not turn the steak. When the timer buzzes, turn the steak with tongs and cook for another 3 minutes. Sprinkle the top with a little salt.

Put the steak onto the plate with the go-withs and cut it in half to bleed out some juice to sauce the bottom of the plate. Pour yourself another glass of good red wine. Cut yourself a bite off the end of the ribeye and enjoy.

Note: If you want to be more Lucullan with this simple dish, drizzle the steak with a little very good olive oil and a squeeze of fresh lemon a moment before serving. Call it Tuscan Steak and open another bottle of Chianti.

Steak Terry Gunn

One of my favorite recipes for good steaks (ribeye, T-bone, or Porterhouse) appeared in a book called *Angler Profiles* (which also set forth the world's best fried fish recipe—mine). It was submitted by a fly-fishing guide and tackle shop owner in Arizona named Terry Gunn. Terry says to start with a steak thicker than 1 inch and to cook it on a flat iron surface, such as a griddle or skillet bottom. The flat surface, he says, and I agree, seals in the juices better than ribbed surfaces. The ingredients are as simple as can be, with the reader given the option of choosing his own seasoning salt.

prime-cut thick steak
Lawry's (or other) seasoning salt

Pat the steak with your favorite seasoning salt. Heat the skillet to the hottest possible point, Gunn says. Sear the steak on both sides, then reduce the heat by 20 percent. Turn the steak frequently—at least once every minute. (Frequent turning will help keep the juices in the middle of the steak instead of letting them drip out, Gunn goes on.) Press on the steak with your finger to determine the level of doneness, Gunn says. I say it takes a total of 3 minutes on each side for a steak that is 1½ inches thick. Then let it coast a little before serving. So . . . there you have it: the best steak that you have ever tasted, Gunn insists. I consider this to be a good way to cook a steak in camp, where a little smoke from the sear won't alarm the local fire department.

Two-Skillet Stroganoff

A number of recipes exist for beef Stroganoff, named after a Russian diplomat, and most of them are suitable for cooking in a skillet. Some experts say that the real stuff does not contain mushrooms or tomatoes in any form. I'll opt for the mushrooms, but the tomatoes are rather late additions to the dish and are therefore questionable on historical grounds. Moreover, Stroganoff is usually served with rice pilaf as well as with noodles and hot boiled new potatoes. (I'll take mine over noodles, thank you.) All of the recipes, however, must contain sour cream, and most are made with very tender beef, usually loin or tenderloin.

1½ pounds beef tenderloin

8 ounces sliced mushrooms

1 cup beef stock or water with bouillon

½ cup sour cream

¼ cup butter or more (divided)

1 medium onion, minced

2 tablespoons whole-wheat flour

1 tablespoon dry bread crumbs

salt and freshly ground black pepper to taste

rice, egg noodles, or new potatoes, cooked separately

Cut the beef into strips about ¼ inch wide. Roll these in flour and set aside. Heat about half the butter in a 10-inch skillet and sauté the mushrooms and onions. Set aside. Heat the rest of the butter in another skillet and quickly brown the beef strips, cooking a few strips at a time.

In the large skillet combine all the browned beef strips with the mushrooms and onions. Add the beef stock and bread crumbs, along with some salt and pepper to taste. Simmer, covered, until the meat is tender, or about 10 minutes, adding more stock or water if needed.

Add the sour cream and bring to a quick boil. Remove from the heat and serve, quite hot, with rice, boiled new potatoes, or noodles, sprinkled with parsley or chopped fresh dill. Feeds 4 to 6. Forget the vodka, but I'll take a little red wine with my serving.

Note: Excellent Stroganoff can also be made from tenderloin of bison, deer, or other big game, such as bear.

Veal Parmigiana

Here's a dish I like to cook with veal cutlets or venison tenderloin, a strip of meat found on the inside of the backbone. (As described at the end of Chapter 5, the twin tenderloins of deer can and should be removed during field dressing, making them a good choice for deer camp cookery. No aging or marinade is required. Like veal, the tenderloin doesn't have much flavor, but—also like veal—it responds well to the coating of Parmesan cheese, which is best when hard, aged, and freshly grated.) It's customary to pound veal cutlets about ¾ inch thick down to about ¼ inch thickness, or less. To clarify butter for the recipe, see Chapter 12. You can also cook this with pork loin cutlets, or with any tender venison steak.

1 to 2 pounds ¾-inch veal cutlets, pounded
½ cup clarified butter
1 cup fine dry bread crumbs
1 cup freshly grated Parmesan cheese
2 chicken eggs
a little water or milk
½ teaspoon dried basil (optional)
salt and black pepper to taste
tomato sauce or salsa (optional)

Mix the bread crumbs, grated Parmesan, salt, pepper, and basil on a sheet of plastic wrap or aluminum foil. Dredge the cutlets in the mixture one at a time and shake off the excess. Lightly whisk the chicken eggs in a bowl with a little water or milk. Dip the cutlets in the beaten egg, letting the excess drip off. Then dredge the cutlets again in the bread crumb mixture. Let sit at room temperature for about 20 minutes, but do not chill.

Heat the clarified butter in a skillet and fry the cutlets, two or three at a time, for about 2 minutes on each side, or until brown and crisp. Serve hot with a tomato sauce or tomato-based salsa (mild, medium, or hot) of your choice, or try it plain if you relish the pronounced flavor of good Parmesan.

Finger-Licking Pork Chops

Prime T-bone pork chops are best for this recipe, but boneless loin chops will also work.

fresh pork T-bones
flour
chicken egg
peanut oil
salt and black pepper to taste
water

Mix some salt and pepper into a little flour. Whisk the chicken egg in a wide, shallow bowl. Flop the pork chops, one at a time, in the egg and dredge in the seasoned flour.

Heat half an inch of peanut oil in a skillet on medium high. Fry the chops, one or two at a time, depending on the size of the skillet, until nicely browned and cooked through. Drain on a brown bag.

Pour off most of the grease and deglaze the skillet with a little water. Add a little flour, stirring constantly with a wooden spoon, and cook until the gravy is the way you want it.

Serve with mashed potatoes, vegetables, and bread. Because pork chops can be on the tough side, a steak knife is recommended for cutting these chops on the plate. Better yet (unless you are feeding snooty guests), simply eat them hand to mouth, a technique that eliminates a lot of work and facilitates the gnawing of the T-bone.

Bornean Pig Chops

Here's a culinary treat that I found in (and adapted from) Richard Sterling's book *Dining with Headhunters*. Sterling, in turn, got it from a native of the jungle called Eetwat, who foraged and processed wild pepper. Wild pigs, I understand, abound in the jungles of Borneo, feeding on local fruits. Highly prized as table fare, they are hunted by the rather nomadic Punan peoples with poisoned dart and blowgun. Anyhow, I tried Eetwat's recipe with loin chops from a Florida pineywood rooter; green peppercorns from a local supermarket (bottled in brine); the juice of two large Parson Brown oranges (a variety developed on Timucuan Island in Lake Weir, where I once lived); peanut oil from the Wiregrass area of Alabama, where I was raised on a peanut farm; and wild onions that grow profusely along the roadways of North America. Use chops from a domestic pig if you must, cutting them about 1 inch thick, and try scallions with green tops in lieu of wild onions—or ramps, in season.

2 pounds loin chops

juice of 2 oranges

¼ cup sliced scallions or wild onions with part of tops

¼ cup green peppercorns, crushed

¼ cup peanut oil

2 cups flour

2 tablespoons salt

2 tablespoons black pepper

Mix the flour, salt, and black pepper in a brown bag. Shake the chops to coat all sides. Heat the peanut oil in a large cast-iron skillet. Brown on both sides, cooking in two or more batches if necessary. Remove the chops, putting them on a brown bag to drain.

Sauté the scallions for 5 or 6 minutes. Place the chops back into the skillet, add the orange juice, cover, and simmer until the chops are almost done (still pink inside).

Remove the chops, add the crushed green peppercorns, and reduce the pan liquid until you have a nice sauce. Pour the sauce over the chops, let sit for a minute or two, and serve with rice and steamed vegetables of your choice.

Leftover Roast Beef Hash

Roast beef from the rump end, usually cooked in an oven or large pot, is likely to be rather dry, especially the second time around. It can be sliced thinly and used in sandwiches, preferably with lots of mayonnaise, or it can be reworked in a moist hash. In this recipe, the meat and vegetables are all cut into a ½-inch dice. The amounts of each ingredient don't have to be exact. The hash also works with leftover venison, buffalo, and so on.

1½ cup diced leftover roast
1½ cups diced potatoes
1 cup diced onion
¾ cup diced green bell pepper
¾ cup diced red bell pepper
¼ cup minced fresh parsley
¼ cup butter
salt and freshly ground pepper
hot water
flour (if wanted)

Heat the butter in a large skillet and brown the onion. Add the red and green bell peppers, parsley, and potatoes. Cook for a few minutes, stirring a time or two. Add the diced beef, salt, and pepper. Heat through. If you want more gravy, as for serving over rice or pasta, stir in a little flour and water. Serve hot.

   Note: If you have some of this hash left over, reheat it the next day with more water or stock and call it a slumgullion, a stew, instead of a hash.

Kansas City Trout

Although the cowboy enjoyed fresh trout whenever he came across a mountain stream, he usually had to settle for fried salt pork, often called overland trout or Kansas City trout. I suppose it would quickly become old, but the fact is that salt pork was very important to the cowboy because it could be eaten boiled, fried, or broiled over the campfire. It can even be eaten raw, if properly cured. I like to eat it from time to time, and find it to be a practical addition to my camp larder. Here's my recipe.

slab of salt pork
stone-ground cornmeal or flour
cayenne
cooking oil
water

Slice the salt pork into strips the length of small trout and between ⅛ and ⅜ inch thick. Simmer the strips in water for about 20 minutes. Drain the strips. Season the cornmeal with cayenne, using 1 or more teaspoons of cayenne per cup of meal. Shake the strips in seasoned cornmeal and fry in a little fat or cooking oil until nicely browned and crisp. Eat hot with biscuits or cornbread.

Note: I gave this recipe to a book editor friend of mine who lives in New England, and he says he cooks it for himself every time his wife leaves town for a few days!

CHAPTER 3

Burger
in the Skillet

**Bulgarian Burgers, Easy Skillet Chili,
Hamburger Steaks for Two,
and Other Ground Meat Recipes,
along with Plans A, B, and C**

Ground meats are frequently cooked in a
skillet, either as patties or meatballs, or loose in such recipes
as chili and spaghetti sauce. The modern cook now has several ground meat choices from the larger supermarkets, including ground beef chuck, ground beef round, ground turkey,
ground pork, ground lamb, and so on.

I normally prefer to purchase market-grind meats—those
that are prepared on location in the store—to prepackaged
meats ground and packaged at another place, often hundreds

of miles away, requiring more handling and time in distribution and more large-batch exposure to contaminants. But with a market grind much depends on the individual store and the butcher, it seems to me. I'm talking about freshness, fat content, and meat scraps, in addition to contamination. Thus, I prefer to deal with a personal butcher in a shop that specializes in meat.

The best bet, however, is to prepare your own burger meat. That way you'll at least know what you have. Here are some talking points.

Sausage Mills. I highly recommend that the cook purchase one of the several electric or hand-cranked sausage mills that are on the market these days. The food processors and other high-speed zappers may work, but I don't want to risk making a mush of good meat. The sausage mills go slower and produce a more uniform grind. It's best to start with large chunks of meat and grind it shortly before it is needed. (This will produce a fresher grind, more likely to be free of harmful contaminants.) Cut the big chunks into 1-inch cubes and grind in a sausage mill fitted with a $\frac{3}{16}$-inch wheel. Finer or coarser grinds can be obtained with different-size wheels. My book *Sausage* sets forth more advice on this matter, along with some sausage recipes suitable for the skillet.

Mixing the Burger. Do not overwork the mixture when adding bread crumbs, chicken egg, spices, or other ingredients. The mix ought not to be smooth or too dense. If adding spices to the mix, let it sit for about 30 minutes to absorb the flavors.

Shaping the Pattie. It's best to shape burger patties by hand—but don't press them tightly. Preshaped burgers or those made in a kitchen press are all right, but I really prefer to make my own the way I want them. Each burger should be a little different. Most of the market patties are too thin for my liking. They are also too geometric—either too perfectly round or square.

Cooking the Burger. Many jackleg chefs and short-order cooks press on a burger with a spatula as it cooks in a skillet or on a griddle. The idea is to press out the red juices, making the burger seem to cook quicker. Although I am guilty of the practice from time to time, I know better. If you want a juicy burger, do not compress the meat during mixing, while shaping the pattie, or during cooking. Period.

Browning the Meat. In preparing such recipes as spaghetti sauce, chili, and so on, many recipe writers instruct the reader to begin by browning the burger meat. While the instruction is clear enough to most of us, the term "brown" is not accurate. Gray would be the better term, but its use as verb would take most readers aback instead of clarifying the matter. In any case, the purpose of "browning" hamburger meat is not, as a rule, to change the color or to partly cook it; instead, the process separates the meat grinds and thereby helps keep it from cooking in chunks.

Some people add a little oil to a skillet before browning the meat, but this is usually not necessary, especially if a rather fat meat is used in the grind, such as beef chuck. Others will take pains to pour out any fat after the meat has been browned. I prefer to use a little water instead of oil to help start the meat without sticking. It works nicely, cooks away, and doesn't increase the fat content.

Hamburger Steaks for Two

As I write these words, I realize that I don't really have a recipe to follow. After further pondering, I decide that I don't want one, either. That way each batch of burgers is something of a culinary adventure, depending in part on the ingredients I have at hand. If I have scallions or spring onions in the garden, for example, some of these will surely find their way, finely chopped, either into the burger pattie or into the gravy, or both. In any case, the gravy is the key to the burger—and the technique of cooking the meat a little longer in the gravy yields a well-done burger that is still moist and succulent on the inside as compared to a overly fried burger or one that has been grilled too long.

In any case, the ingredients below are for starters. You'll also need a 10-inch cast-iron skillet for these measures. (Ideally, the steak pattie should almost fill the skillet and should also be about 1½ inches in thickness.) Ground chuck, which usually contains just the right amount of fat, is recommended, but other meats can also be used. If the meat is very dry, add a couple of strips of bacon, finely minced, to the mix. Note that no egg or other goo is added to the meat, which means that the pattie will have to be handled gently so that it won't break apart.

1 pound ground chuck
½ cup minced onion
½ cup minced mushrooms
2 cloves garlic, minced (more or less)
2 tablespoons Worcestershire sauce
flour
salt and freshly ground black pepper
cooking oil
a little water or wine

Mix some salt, black pepper, and Worcestershire sauce into the ground meat, using your hands. Shape the burger into a pattie that will fit nicely into the skillet. Cook the burger in about ⅛ inch oil for about 10 minutes on medium high, then turn and cook the other side. (It should be lightly browned on both sides, but try to accomplish this without much turning and flopping over.) Cut the pattie in half right across the middle. Using a spatula, carefully lift one half and fit it atop the other, still in the pan. (This will give you half a skillet free for making the gravy.)

Tilt the skillet and spoon out most of the grease. Reduce the tilt a little and add the onion and mushrooms. Cook for 4 or 5 minutes, then add the garlic. Cook for 2 minutes, stirring as you go. Add a little flour to the skillet and stir it about with a wooden spoon, as when making a roux. Slowly pour in about ¼ cup water or red wine, or both, stirring and shaking the skillet. At this point, using two spatulas or one spatula and your hand, carefully reverse the pattie stack, putting the top half right into the gravy. Tilt the skillet a little to get some gravy all around, then put the top pattie down. Spoon a little gravy over all, cover, lower the heat, and simmer for 4 or 5 minutes, lifting the skillet off the burner from time to time to reduce the chance of scorching the bottom.

Serve a pattie on each plate, topped with some of the gravy. Serve with mashed potatoes or rice, more gravy, and vegetables of your choice, with some good red wine.

Note: As stated above, this recipe changes just about every time I cook it. For a variation made with black coffee in the gravy, see my book *Cast-Iron Cooking*.

Versatile Venison Burgers

Burgers made from ground venison without added fat are quite tasty, but they can be on the dry side and tend to come apart during cooking and turning. Here's an easy recipe for keeping them succulent and intact. I don't offer exact measurements, but anybody who has ever made hamburgers won't have much trouble. It's best not to crowd the burgers in the skillet, cooking in more than one batch if need be. For practice, go one burger at a time in a small skillet.

freshly ground venison
cream of mushroom soup
finely minced onion
dry red wine (optional)
a little vegetable oil or spray
salt and freshly ground black pepper
hamburger buns

Mix the onion, salt, and black pepper into the ground venison, along with a little of the mushroom soup. Shape the mixture into loose patties about ¾ inch thick. Heat a skillet and add a little oil, or spray, to keep the burgers from sticking. Cook the burgers on medium heat for about 5 minutes. Turn carefully with a thin spatula and cook for another 4 minutes. (I often use two spatulas, placing one on top of the burger to help hold it together on the turn.)

Add some of the mushroom soup to the skillet, using a tablespoon to place it around the sides of the burgers and on top. Use a generous amount of the soup—enough to give you half an inch (or a little better) of liquid in the skillet. Add a little red wine, if you have any left. Cover and simmer on very low heat for 5 minutes. Turn carefully and simmer for another 5 minutes, adding a little more soup or red wine if needed. Carefully remove the burgers and place them on hamburger buns, topping with a little of the pan gravy, thinly sliced onion, a sprinkle of grated cheese, thin tomato slices, sautéed mushrooms, or whatever you like on your burgers.

Plan B. If your burgers don't hold together, break up the patties in the skillet, add more mushroom soup, and spread the mix over open-faced hamburger buns. Call the mess Pete's Sloppy Joes if your name is Pete—or Joe's Sloppy Petes if your name is Joe—and serve proudly, without letting on that the dish is a failed burger.

Plan C. If you are feeding sophisticated folks, spoon the venison and soup mix over egg noodles instead of hamburger buns. Add a dollop of sour cream and call it Russian Venison Stroganoff. If you want to eat French instead of Russian and have some more wine, use crème fraîche instead of ordinary sour cream and serve over pasta (al dente, of course) with a chunk of chewy bread on the side. Red wine all around.

Russian Meat Patties

Said to split the difference between an American hamburger and a Swedish meatball, a Russian specialty called kotlety is served up with a sauce called podlivka. There are many versions of both sauce and pattie. This recipe, making use of sour cream, is adapted from Kira Petrovskaya's *Russian Cookbook*. It can be cooked in any good skillet, and is ideal for large electric skillets.

1½ pounds lean chunks beef
1 medium to large onion
2 or 3 slices stale white bread
dry bread crumbs
butter (used twice)
2 tablespoons sour cream
1 chicken egg lightly whisked
a little milk
salt and pepper to taste
2 or 3 tablespoons water

Trim the crust off the bread. Soak the bread in a little milk for a few minutes, then squeeze it out and set aside. Cut the meat into small chunks and run through a meat grinder with a medium or fine blade (no larger than ³⁄₁₆ inch). Mix in the stale bread, squash the mix all together with your fingers, and run it through the grinder again. Add the grated onion, salt, pepper, and chicken egg, stirring as you go with a wooden spoon.

Heat the skillet to medium hot. Add about ¼ cup of butter. As the butter heats, shape the meat mixture into small balls or ovals, somewhat smaller than the typical hamburger. Roll the balls in dry bread crumbs, then flatten them loosely with a chef's knife, making patties instead of balls. Cut a crisscross on either side. Cook the patties a few at a time in the butter for 4 or 5 minutes, then turn carefully and cook for another 4 minutes or so. (Overcrowding the skillet will make them difficult to turn.) Put the cooked patties on a hot platter or plate. Cook the rest of the batch, adding more butter as needed.

When all the patties have been browned, turn the heat to high and add a little fresh butter to the skillet along with 2 or 3 tablespoons of water, stirring and scraping any tidbits (grimilles) off the bottom of the skillet. Reduce the heat and stir in 2 tablespoons of sour cream. Pour the sauce over the patties and serve hot. Feeds 4 to 6 ordinary people—or 2 Russians.

Bulgarian Burgers

I found this recipe in Atanas Slavov's book *Traditional Bulgarian Cooking*. It is typical of the almost infinite ways that different kinds of ground meats can be mixed. Try ground venison burger instead of lamb.

2 pounds ground lamb
1 pound ground beef
2 medium onions, minced
½ cup chopped fresh parsley
2 chicken eggs
1 slice white bread
4 teaspoons flour
1 tablespoon butter (more as needed)
½ teaspoon cumin
salt and freshly ground black pepper to taste
warm water

Remove the crust from the bread and give it to the dog. Soak the bread in a little water for a few minutes. Squeeze out the bread, shred it, and place it into a large bowl. Mix in the meat, eggs, spices, onions, and parsley, along with ¼ cup of water. Use your hands to squash and knead the mixture, then shape it into 8 burgers about 3 inches wide and 1 inch thick.

Place the flour in a plate and carefully set each burger in it. Turn the burger to coat both sides and shake off any excess flour. (Add more flour to the plate if needed.) Heat the butter on medium-high heat and cook each burger for about 4 minutes on each side. Use more butter if needed.

These burgers can be eaten as a meat pattie, perhaps topped with mushroom sauce or gravy made in the skillet. The patties also work as a bun filler, using as your would a regular burger. The flour will give the burger a little different texture, however, so consider using a little more mayonnaise or other condiment than usual.

Seminole Burgers

The Seminole Indians made a bread of pumpkin and flour, as discussed in Chapter 9. This dough was rolled out flat and fried, but sometimes they used rounds of dough to encase meat patties. Then the whole thing was fried. Ground beef, venison, or other good red meat can be used.

2 pounds ground red meat
½ cup minced onion
salt and black pepper to taste
1 recipe Seminole Pumpkin Bread dough (Chapter 9)
cooking oil

Mix the ground meat, onion, salt, and black pepper. Shape into 6 patties. Roll out 6 rounds of dough about twice as wide as the burgers. Put a burger into each round of dough, fold in the edges, and pinch shut.

Heat an inch or so of oil in a skillet. Fry each burger until golden brown, turning several times. Serve hot. These are easy to hold and easy to eat, making them ideal for feeding children in camp.

One-Skillet Dinner

Many are the recipes for cooking a whole meal in a single pot or even a skillet, and many people cook up some such dish without following a recipe, depending on what we have at hand that needs using up. A lot of these recipes call for ground meat, partly because it's easy to use, readily available, and liked by almost everyone except vegetarians and vegans. A large skillet with a lid is usually best, and a square electric skillet is ideal. Here's a recipe for openers, but remember that exact measures aren't necessary. In other words, you can dice up a medium onion without measuring to see whether or not it makes exactly 1 cup.

1 pound hamburger meat
2 cups diced celery with part of green tops
2 cups diced potatoes
1 cup diced onion
½ cup diced red bell pepper
½ cup diced green bell pepper (or jalapeño)
½ cup diced mushrooms
salt and freshly ground black pepper
water or beef stock

Add a little water or beef stock to the skillet, then brown the meat and onion, stirring as you go with a wooden spoon. Add the potatoes, celery, bell peppers, and mushrooms, along with salt and pepper and some more water. Reduce the heat to a simmer, cover tightly, and cook for 20 minutes or so. Serve hot. A loaf of bread completes the meal.

Easy Skillet Chili

Here's a recipe that I like to cook in a cast-iron skillet whenever I want only a small batch of chili or do not have a large pot handy.

For the cracklings, cut the salt pork into slices down to the rind. Then cut the slices into ¼-inch dice. Discard the rind, or use it to make your own pork rind for fishing. (Simply place the rind in highly salted water and store in the refrigerator. Cut into strips, or perhaps frog-shaped chunks.)

Regular ground beef can be used, but a coarse grind works better. I like to use chuck ground with a ½ inch-wheel. If you can't simmer the chili for at least 2 hours, however, use a regular hamburger grind. The chile powder used in the recipe does not contain spices and should not be confused with chili powder.

2 pounds chili-grind beef
2 ounces salt pork
¼ cup minced onion
2 cloves garlic, minced
4 tablespoons pure chile powder (ancho or New Mexico)
1 tablespoon freshly ground cumin seeds
¼ teaspoon dried Mexican oregano
salt and freshly ground black pepper to taste
water or beef stock

Cook the salt pork in a large skillet until the pieces give up most of their fat and are crispy. Drain the cracklings and set aside, resisting the temptation to eat one or two.

Brown the ground beef in the skillet. Stir in the onion and garlic. Sprinkle on the chile powder, cumin, oregano, pepper, and salt. Add enough water or beef stock to barely cover and stir well. Heat almost to a boil, then reduce the heat and simmer for 2 hours or longer, uncovered. Stir and taste from time to time with a wooden spoon, adding more liquid as needed.

Toward the end, cook down until the chili is quite thick. Serve in bowls, topping each serving off with a dollop of sour cream and a sprinkling of the cracklings.

A.D.'s Pasta Helper Meatballs

The best spaghetti sauces are simmered for hours in a cast-iron pot or large skillet, stirred from time to time with a wooden spoon. Recipes abound, and most cooks will have a family favorite or otherwise will brown some burger meat and pour in a can or two of prepared tomato-based sauce. Here's a quick variation, without tomato, that I like to make.

1 pound hamburger meat
1 small can cream of mushroom soup
fettuccine (or similar pasta or egg noodles)
bacon drippings or cooking oil (olive oil will do)
salt and black pepper to taste
Chianti

Cook the fettuccine according to the directions on the package, preferably al dente. Using your hands, squash some salt and pepper into the burger meat. Shape the meat into small balls—no larger than 1 inch across—and set them aside on a flat surface. (The balls should hold their shape nicely but should not be compressed.)

Heat about ¾ inch of oil in a skillet. Put some meatballs into the skillet but do not overcrowd them. Fry for a few minutes, turning a time or two, until nicely browned. Drain the balls on a brown bag. Repeat until all the meatballs have been fried.

Pour the oil out of the skillet and deglaze with a little Chianti. Stir in the can of mushroom soup. Add the meatballs back to the skillet. Cook for a few minutes more, stirring constantly but gently. Fill each plate with hot fettuccine and top generously with meatballs and gravy. Serve hot with some chewy Italian bread, a colorful tossed salad, and some more Chianti.

Note: A topping of freshly grated Parmesan cheese goes nicely with this dish.

CHAPTER 4

Birds
in the Skillet

The World's Best Fried Chicken,
Turkey Fingers,
Skillet Duck with Muscadine Jelly,
Mexican Skillet Doves,
and Other Recipes for
Domestic and Wild Fowl

I have included a few hunter's birds here instead of putting them in the chapter on game, partly because many of these, such as quail and pheasant and mallards, are farm- or pen-raised these days, either for home consumption or for marketing in our supermarkets, or for sale by mail-order. Other fowl, such as the guinea hen, are available and may even be regional barnyard favorites. Although this approach opens the doors to almost limitless and tempting culinary adventure, there are practical limits to the coverage in a book like this. Reluctantly, I've decided not to include recipes for the very large birds such as ostrich and emu, which are usually compared to beef, not chicken. Nor do I include very many recipes for duck or goose, simply because these are better (as a rule) when roasted in the oven instead of cooked in the skillet on top of the stove.

Fact is, chicken is the main bird for these times, at least in North America. So, let's get on with it.

Skillet-Fried Chicken

You don't need a long list of secret spices to fry good chicken. Salt and black pepper will do, preferably fine sea salt and freshly ground black pepper. You don't even need a deep fryer or a "chicken fryer." A 10- or 12-inch cast-iron skillet will do—and may be better if you insist, as I do, on having the bottom of the chicken in contact with the bottom of the pan. You do need good chicken, a whole bird, preferably from the barnyard or at least "free range" style. Many modern cooks, accustomed to buying supermarket bird parts and fast-food fare, won't know how to pluck and cut up a bird properly, and probably won't even recognize some of the best parts, such as the pully bone and the back.

Most modern housewives or even jackleg cooks aren't going to catch their own bird, wring its neck, pluck it, and singe it. But it's still easy to purchase a whole fryer, plucked and drawn, in the supermarket. For best results, cut it into the following pieces: two drumsticks, two thighs, one back, one pully bone (cut from the front of the breast), two breast halves, two wings, one rib assembly (we used to call it the crag in my family), one neck, and, sometimes, one head, along with a liver, gizzard, and heart, if these parts are included with the bird, as they damn well ought to be. If you proceed with an unplucked farmyard bird, note that the gizzard, an ovoid-shaped organ, should be split along one side and turned inside out, dumping the contents. I read in a cookbook on British country cooking that the two gizzards should be separated, but, unfortunately, most American birds have only one gizzard.

Having such a variety of pieces, all crisply fried and piled on a platter in the center of the table, is part of the whole chicken experience. Each family member will have favorite parts, and sometimes the head of the table must be firm to maintain order and manners. In most families, the breast is usually reserved for any guest at the table. The pully bone goes to one of the kids.

For the best skillet fry, use a cast-iron piece and fill it with about ¾ inch of peanut oil. The oil should almost but not quite cover the chicken pieces. This works much better than a deep-fry method simply because the bottom of the chicken will be in direct contact with the bottom of the skillet. This in turn will produce a well-browned spot, one on either side, a feature that is not obtained when deep-frying.

Note also that the best chicken is not covered during the frying process. This will allow the chicken to crisp up nicely. If covered, the bird will be partly steamed and not as crusty. Yeah, yeah, I know. An uncovered skillet will spatter a little grease onto the stove, thereby making a mess. If that will cause a problem in your household, maybe between the cook and whoever has to clean the stove, you might consider rigging a stove on the patio or in the tool shed. One of my neighbors has a cook shed in the backyard where he retreats to fry both chicken and fish, as well as for making cracklings.

The recipe for the world's best chicken? Well, it need not have a long list of ingredients. Here's all you'll need.

1 fryer, cut up
all-purpose flour
fine sea salt and freshly ground black pepper
peanut oil

Sprinkle the chicken pieces with salt and pepper, then shake a few pieces in a bag with some flour. Using your fingers, shake off the excess flour, and set the pieces aside.

Heat about ¾ inch of peanut oil in a cast-iron skillet until it starts to quiver. Hold a drumstick by the small end and touch the big end into the oil. If it sizzles, it's hot enough (about 350° or 360°F if you have a thermometer handy). Put several pieces into the skillet, being careful not to overcrowd. Cook for about 8 minutes or so. Using tongs, lift up a piece to see how it looks. If crisply brown, turn to cook the other side. Note that each piece should be considered separately because thicker pieces take longer to cook and don't brown as quickly. Be careful when frying the liver; it may pop and splatter hot grease on you.

As soon as a piece is ready, lift it from the skillet and put it on a brown bag to drain. (Paper towels will work, but large brown bags are better.) Do not cover. Cook the rest of the batch and serve hot on a large platter. Help yourself. I'll take the back, the liver, and one of the wings, to start with.

Fried chicken goes best with mashed potatoes and gravy, peas and other vegetables, and hot biscuits or rolls.

Creole Fried Chicken

Here's an old New Orleans recipe, made without the highly spiced Cajun dust that we see in many modern creations from that important part of the culinary world.

1 fryer (2 to 2½ pounds)
1½ cups fine cracker meal
½ cup flour
2 chicken eggs
milk
salt and white pepper
peanut oil

Cut the chicken into conventional serving pieces. (If you must, substitute breasts, thighs, and so on, prepackaged from the supermarket.) Sprinkle the pieces with salt and white pepper. Whisk the egg, a little milk, and a pinch of salt in a small bowl. Pour the egg wash over the chicken and let it stand for an hour or so, mixing from time to time.

When you are ready to proceed, heat about an inch of peanut oil in a skillet to medium hot. Mix the cracker meal and flour, then roll each piece of chicken in the mixture, shaking off the excess. Fry the chicken a few pieces at a time for about 12 to 15 minutes, or until each piece is done. Serve hot.

Mushroom Smothered Chicken

This is essentially a fried chicken with a mushroom and butter sauce poured over it during the last stage of cooking. I've included a list of ingredients, but it's easy to come up with your own ways and means for this one. Cut the chicken into legs, thighs, split breast, wings, back, neck, and bony pieces. The back and bony pieces can be saved for chicken soup or stock—but remember, these make for good gnawing at the table. The recipe works best with two skillets, as indicated below, but one skillet will do if you cook the mushrooms first and set them aside until needed.

1 fryer cut into pieces

12 ounces mushrooms, sliced

1 cup butter

½ cup red wine

peanut oil for skillet frying

all-purpose flour

salt and freshly ground black pepper

warm water

Salt and pepper the chicken pieces. Put some flour into a bag and shake the chicken a few pieces at a time until nicely coated. Shake off the excess flour piece by piece and set aside.

Heat about an inch of peanut oil in a 10-inch or larger skillet. Fry the chicken, a few pieces at a time, on medium-high heat until the chicken is nicely browned all around. Drain on a brown bag.

While the chicken cooks, melt the butter in another skillet and sauté the mushrooms on medium heat for 10 minutes or so. When all the chicken has been fried, pour off the grease and deglaze the skillet with the red wine. Put the chicken pieces back into the skillet. Add the rest of the red wine and enough water to almost cover the chicken. Bring to a boil, reduce the heat to low, and add the sautéed mushrooms and butter from the second skillet. Sprinkle with a little salt and pepper. Cover and simmer for 20 minutes or so, stirring a time or two.

Serve hot, along with rice or mashed potatoes, baby peas, and so on.

Turkey Fingers

Although the breast from domestic turkey will work just fine, this recipe should be remembered as the perfect way to cook wild turkey for those who think they might not like the "wild" part. Truth is, the breast from a wild jake is tenderer and more moist than the typical market turkey. It can also have more flavor, depending in part on what it has been feeding on. Here's what you'll need:

turkey fingers (cut from the breast lengthwise)
buttermilk
flour
cooking oil
salt
pepper

Rinse the turkey fingers, put them into a glass container, cover with buttermilk, and refrigerate for several hours or overnight. When you are ready to start cooking, drain the turkey fingers, salt and pepper them to taste, and shake them in a bag with some flour. Heat ½ inch of cooking oil in a skillet. Fry all the fingers a few at the time on medium-high heat, turning once, and put them onto a brown grocery bag to drain. Use more than one brown bag if necessary to avoid piling the fingers atop each other. Eat while hot.

The breast from a fully grown wild turkey will usually feed 5 or 6. But wild turkey can be delicious, and, if you've done a proper job of field dressing and cooking, your squeamish guest can eat more than expected.

Note: This recipe also comes in handy for cooking chicken tenders, which don't need long soaking in buttermilk, and pheasant fingers, which should be soaked a little longer. Pheasant breast tends to be quite dry, so do not overcook it. As a rule, a young pheasant or a hen will fry up better than a tough old rooster—which also holds true for chickens.

Gullah Maa'sh Hen

Hunting marsh hens (usually clapper rails) and other coastal birds has long been a Low Country specialty. At one time, a number of species could be taken for the table, such as the delicious limpkin and the beautiful purple gallinule, but these days the legal bounty is restricted. Other small birds such as snipe and mourning doves can be used in this recipe, but check the latest game laws before working up an appetite.

8 marsh hens or snipe
1 chopped onion
1 cup vinegar
cooking oil
flour
salt
red pepper flakes

Skin the marsh hens to help remove any fishy taste. Draw and soak them in about a quart of clean saltwater, using either ocean water or fresh water with salt added. Change the saltwater, add the vinegar, and let sit in a cool place overnight.

When you are ready to cook, drain the birds, sprinkle with salt, and dredge in flour. Fry them in about ½ inch of hot oil in a large skillet until nicely browned on both sides. Pour off most of the oil, then add the onion and red pepper flakes. Stir in a cup of fresh water, cover the pan, and simmer on very low heat until the birds are tender.

Serve with rice and steamed young okra pods (another Gullah specialty) or vegetables of your choice.

Skillet Doves

I have eaten more doves than any other kind of game bird, partly because I like the rich dark meat—which I find even better than breast of duck. There are several types, such as mourning doves and white-wings, but most are similar except for a little variation in size. Pigeons are larger and should not be cooked by this recipe. Ground doves are smaller and are protected by law these days.

Whoever dresses the birds has a good deal of control over the quality of the final product and often does the wrong thing because it is easier than doing the right thing. If your wife always dresses the birds, tell her that doves ought to be dry-plucked. Skinning them (as too many people do) will make them drier and tougher. Breasting the birds is widely accepted, but I really can't in good conscience endorse the practice unless the bony parts will be used, along with the giblets, to make a giblet gravy. Cooking the birds whole in a skillet isn't the best way to go either. For best results, pluck and draw the birds, then halve them lengthwise, cutting close to the breastbone. Use no marinade if you want to savor the flavor of my favorite game bird.

doves, halved
peanut oil
flour
salt and freshly ground black pepper

Sprinkle the bird halves with salt and pepper, dredge with flour, and shake off the excess. Set aside while you heat an inch of peanut oil in a skillet. When the oil starts to quiver with heat, cook the birds 2 or 3 pieces at a time until browned nicely on both sides. Drain and cook another batch, repeating until all the birds are done.

Serve hot with mashed potatoes, gravy, vegetables, and a good bread. Eat the birds with your hands. First, gnaw off a few bites of the breast meat. Then gnaw on the bony pieces as best you can, nibbling and pulling with your fingers. Allow at least 2 doves per person. I'll take 3 or 4 if available, or nibbling rights to whatever bony pieces the other diners leave.

Note: Snipe, woodcock, and other small birds can be cooked by the same recipe, but remember that doves are grain eaters that do not have a strong off-flavor. Other birds may require a marinade of some sort, as in the marsh hen recipe above.

Mexican Skillet Doves

Doves are quite plentiful in parts of Mexico, where hundreds can still be bagged in a single shoot. A number of Mexican recipes can be used to cook them, sometimes using half a dozen kinds of chile pepper. This recipe, however, is very easy, using ingredients available in any supermarket north of the border. Pluck and draw the birds, removing feet and heads. Cook them whole, without splitting or disjointing. You'll need a rather deep skillet with a tightly fitting lid. A "chicken fryer" or an electric skillet will be great.

6 to 8 doves
1 cup prepared tomato-based salsa
1 tablespoon brown sugar
flour
salt and black pepper to taste
cooking oil
water

Salt and pepper the birds, then dredge with flour inside and out. Heat an inch of cooking oil in the skillet. Brown the birds a few at a time and set aside to drain.

Pour off most of the cooking oil and deglaze the skillet with a little water. Add the salsa and brown sugar. Cook and stir for about 5 minutes. Put the birds back into the skillet, fitting them in nicely and spooning some of the salsa over the tops. Add more water to almost cover the birds. Bring to a bubble, reduce the heat, cover tightly, and simmer for 1½ hours, stirring and turning the birds from time to time and adding more water if needed.

Serve with white rice or yellow hominy, a green vegetable, napoles, rolled cornmeal tortillas, and Mexican beer or iced tea.

Smother-Fried Quail

Non-hunters will find market quail, usually frozen, to be quite tasty, and sometimes fresh quail can be purchased from local producers. You'll need a skillet large enough to hold all the birds at one time instead of cooking in batches. I prefer a red wine for this recipe, but white might be the more proper choice. Any good mushroom will do for the gravy, but wild morels are perfect. Chanterelles or shiitakes are also great. Note also that about 2 ounces of dried mushrooms, properly reconstituted, are also very good in this recipe.

8 quail
buttermilk
16 ounces fresh morels or shiitakes
peanut oil for frying
2 cups chicken broth
2 cups dry red wine
1 cup chopped scallions with part of green tops
flour
salt and black pepper

Rinse the dressed quail, put them into a nonmetallic container, and cover with buttermilk. Refrigerate for several hours in the refrigerator, turning a time or two.

When you are ready to cook, drain the birds and pat dry with paper towels. Heat about ¾ inch of peanut oil in a skillet to about 350°F. Sprinkle each bird inside and out with salt and black pepper, then shake in a bag with flour, working one bird at a time. Shake off the excess flour and arrange the birds in the skillet, breast-side down. Cook for 4 or 5 minutes, then turn the birds on their backs. Cook until the birds are nicely browned, then put them aside to drain on a brown bag.

Pour off the oil and pour a little of the wine into the hot skillet, stirring it about and scraping any grimilles off the bottom. Add the rest of the wine, the chicken broth, mushrooms, and green onions, along with a little more salt and pepper, if desired. Add the quail back to the skillet, cover, reduce the heat, and simmer for about 30 minutes. Remove the cover, stir the birds about, and cook until the liquid reduces down to a gravy. Be careful not to burn the bottom of the birds.

Serve hot with wild rice, steamed vegetables, and a chewy sopping bread. Servings? Allow 2 quail per person. One will do if you will fit in a chicken finger or two.

Skillet Duck with Muscadine Jelly

The Tabasco Cookbook includes a recipe for venison chops with muscadine jelly, calling the result Marchand de Muscadine. A sidebar also sets forth an old recipe for cooking skillet duck with muscadines, a large, tasty grape that grows wild over most of the South. You simply fillet out the breasts of teal or wood ducks (saving the rest of the birds for duck and andouille gumbo). Dip each breast in melted butter and cook in a skillet for about 3½ minutes on each side, or until medium rare. (Be careful. Much depends on the heat of the skillet and the thickness of the fillets. In any case, the breasts should be medium rare.) Salt and pepper each fillet and smear lightly with muscadine jelly. Serve hot with wild rice.

The muscadine jelly can be ordered from Callaway Gardens in Georgia (404–663–5100). It's also easy enough to make your own, if you have the muscadines and the time. If you must, substitute guava or red currant jelly.

My copy of *The Tabasco Cookbook* sports an attractive cover, designed with the title fitted into the familiar Tabasco brand diamond, suggestive of the bottle. With taste buds atingle, I was unprepared for a typographical shock when I first opened my copy, naturally holding it with the cover right-side up. Astoundingly, the last page of the text was at the front—and all the pages were upside down! Maybe Tabasco sauce fans are expected to invert the book and shake out the contents.

Skillet Goose Nuggets

Here's a recipe from Bob Stearns, a noted angling and boating writer, adapted here from *Angler Profiles*. It calls for using only the breast of the goose, leaving the rest for soup or gumbo. The recipe works for both wild and domestic geese, as well as for ducklings and the larger wild ducks such as mallards.

goose breasts
milk
orange juice
1 to 2 chicken eggs
seasoned Italian bread crumbs
olive oil

Fillet out the breasts and cut them into bite-sized pieces. Put these into a glass or plastic container of suitable size and marinate in milk for 12 to 14 hours in a refrigerator. Then rinse and marinate them in orange juice for 3 or 4 hours. Drain the orange juice and mix in a whisked egg or two. Sprinkle with bread crumbs, coating all sides lightly.

Heat a little olive oil in a skillet and sauté the pieces for 2 or 3 minutes on each side. Do not overcook. Servings? An average wild goose breast will serve 2 average people.

CHAPTER 5

Venison and Other Game in the Skillet

Big Scrub Venison, Caribou Stroganoff, Aztec Rabbit, Safari Steaks, and Other Toothsome Bounty from the Hunt and Game Farm

Venison and most other game can be very good eating—or almost inedible. Sometimes the same animal can fulfill either extreme, depending on how it was killed, dressed, and cooked. Usually, game purchased from a game farm or commercial market will be satisfactory—but a lazy or irresponsible hunter is often to blame for gamy-tasting meat being put on the table. As a rule, a young but mature animal will be better eating than a tough old buck, but the real culprit of that gamy taste is improper field dressing. I don't want to preach here, but I'll have more on this subject at the end of the chapter.

Most of the recipes here are for whitetail venison simply because white-tailed deer are so plentiful in most parts of the country, but mule deer, elk, moose, caribou, and similar animals can also be used. Buffalo (bison) is especially good. The first few recipes in this chapter can be cooked in the home kitchen or on the patio, but they are also ideal for deer camp cookery after a successful hunt. This chapter also contains recipes for squirrel and rabbit. (For cooking such critters as coons and possums, see my *Complete Fish & Game Cookbook*.) Wild birds are discussed separately (Chapter 4), and a few other game recipes appear here and there throughout the book.

A Tenderloin Sauté

This recipe works with venison tenderloin of any sort and with most loins. The tenderloins are great for camp cooking after a successful hunt because they can be removed from within the body cavity during the field-dressing operation—before the deer is skinned (see "The Hunter's Responsibility," at the end of this chapter).

1 set whitetail tenderloins, sliced ½ inch thick
3 tablespoons butter (divided)
3 tablespoons chopped green onions with part of tops
salt and freshly ground black pepper

Rub some ground pepper into each side of the tenderloin slices. Heat 2 tablespoons of the butter in a skillet. Sauté the tenderloins for 6 minutes for medium rare, turning once to brown both sides. Sprinkle with salt and set aside to drain on a brown bag.

Add the rest of the butter to the skillet, then sauté the onions for 4 or 5 minutes, stirring as you go. Spoon the onion mixture over the meat rounds. Feeds 2 hunters—maybe more if you have plenty of rice.

Chicken-Fried Loin Chops
with Soption

Dump a cup or so of flour into a small brown bag, along with a little salt and pepper. Shake the chops in the bag, remove, and gently shake off any excess flour.

Pour ½ inch of peanut oil into the skillet and heat it to about 350°F. Fry the loin slices for 2 or 3 minutes, turning once, or until lightly browned on either side. Drain the slices on a brown bag. (Note: If the loin slices prove to be too tough for easy chewing—probably because you have cooked them too long—abort this recipe here at the draining stage and resort to Step B of the next recipe.)

Quickly pour off most of the oil and scrape up any bottom dredgings—the grimilles. Sprinkle a little flour into the skillet and cook for several minutes, stirring with a wooden spoon, until the flour browns. Add a little water, stirring constantly, and bring to a bubble. Sprinkle with some salt and pepper, and simmer, stirring until the gravy thickens to your liking.

Serve the gravy over rice, mashed potatoes, or biscuit halves along with the fried chops.

Smother-Fried Chops

Step A: Flour and fry the chops in hot oil as directed in the recipe above. Drain the cooked slices and pour most of the oil out of the skillet.

Step B: Scrape up any pan dredgings, sprinkle in a little flour, stir about, and then add the fried tenderloin back to the skillet. Pour in enough water or beef stock to cover the chops. Bring to a boil, reduce the heat, cover the skillet tightly, and simmer for 30 minutes or longer, until the pieces are fork tender. Watch the skillet closely, stirring and turning the pieces a time or two and adding a little water as needed. Serve hot, spooning meat and gravy over individual servings of rice or pasta.

Deer Camp Venison Liver

Fresh venison liver is very tasty, unless you find all liver off-putting. I like it cooked with onions and a little port wine. As Cy Littlebee's *Guide to Cooking Fish & Game* put it, the port "not only improves the taste, but the smell is sure to bring in any lost hunters that might be near-by and down-wind." I agree—but the real olfactory magic here is onions sautéing in butter.

Note that other liver, such as calf or chicken, can be used. (See the turtle liver recipe, Higado de Tortuga, in Chapter 7.) Note also that venison liver has no gallbladder attached to it, so that you don't have to worry about it during the field-dressing operation. I like to slice the liver about ½ inch thick. The onion should be halved lengthwise and then cut crosswise into half-rings.

venison liver

bacon

onion half-rings

sliced mushrooms

port wine

flour

salt and freshly ground black pepper

Pour yourself a glass of the port to sip while cooking. Sprinkle the liver with salt, black pepper, and flour. Cook the bacon in a cast-iron skillet until crispy. Drain and set aside.

Sauté the onion rings in the bacon drippings until they start to brown around the edges. (If you burn them a little and have city folks seated at the table, change the name of the recipe to Venison Liver with Caramelized Onions.) Add the mushrooms and cook for a few minutes, stirring a time or two. Remove the onions and mushrooms and set aside. Add a little more bacon drippings (or cooking oil) to the skillet if needed. Fry the liver on medium-high heat for 2 or 3 minutes, or until medium rare. (If in doubt, cut into a slice of the liver for a visual test; it should be brown on the outside but pink on the inside.) Pour some port into the skillet around the liver. Add the onions and mushrooms. Cover and simmer for a minute or two.

Serve hot with the pan gravy, along with rice, vegetables of your choice, and a good crusty bread. Finish off with scuppernong hull pie (or maybe rhubarb pie) and the rest of the port.

Safari Steaks

Used by Kenyan hunters, this recipe specifies eland steaks, but it also works with steaks or chops of antelope, zebra, beef, veal, or buffalo. Any good American deer can be used. In any case, use only tender cuts of meat for this one—and do not overcook them.

2 pounds eland steaks, ½ inch thick
1½ pounds mashed potatoes (precooked)
1 pound mashed sweet potatoes
½ cup dry red wine
½ cup sweet white wine
½ cup tomato sauce
2 tablespoons olive oil (maybe more)
2 tablespoons butter
2 cloves garlic, minced
salt and pepper to taste
chopped fresh parsley (for garnish)

Heat the oil and butter in a skillet almost to the smoke point. Add a small batch of the steaks and cook for 3 minutes on each side. (Do not overcrowd the meat.) Cook the rest of the steaks, using more oil if needed. Salt and pepper the steaks and set aside on a warm platter.

On lower heat now, add the wines and deglaze the skillet, stirring and scraping up the bottom grimilles with a wooden spatula. Add the garlic. Stir in the tomato sauce and simmer, stirring constantly, until the sauce thickens. Keep the sauce warm.

In a suitable bowl mix the mashed potatoes and sweet potatoes, adding a little salt and pepper to taste. Spread the potatoes over a serving platter. Top with the steaks and pour the sauce over all. Serve hot, garnished perhaps with chopped parsley.

Big Scrub Venison

Marjorie Kinnan Rawlings, the author of *The Yearling*, offered a good Florida Cracker recipe for frying venison in *Cross Creek Cookery*, a work that has been in print since 1941. I have used the recipe several times with butterflied tenderloin as well as with top loin chops.

venison chops, ¾ inch thick
lemon halves
butter
Crisco or vegetable oil
flour
salt and pepper

Rub the chops with half a lemon, squeezing on a little juice as you go. Dust each chop with flour and fry it in a cast-iron skillet on medium-high heat, using about 1 tablespoon of butter and 1 tablespoon of Crisco or vegetable oil for medium-sized skillets. (In camp, try bacon drippings leftover from breakfast.) Fry the venison for 5 or 6 minutes, turning once. Salt and pepper to taste and serve hot.

Old Warsaw Stuffed Venison Cutlets

This recipe works with cutlets from venison loin, or from cutlets made from the muscles in the deer's leg. Cut them to about ½ inch thickness, then pound them down with a meat mallet to ¼ inch. The ground meat can be from the shoulder of the animal, or from other tasty cuts. I have adapted the recipe from Rysia's *Old Warsaw Cookbook*, taking the liberty to add a little bacon to the ground meat. Also, the original didn't spell out what to do with the flour—and I have chosen to beat it into the meat. You'll need a cover for your skillet to finish this recipe. An electric skillet will do just fine.

2 pounds venison cutlets
1 pound venison shoulder for grinding
4 strips bacon (divided)
1 medium onion, minced
4 mushrooms, minced
½ cup good red wine
½ cup meat stock
1 bouillon cube, dissolved in a little water
butter (preferably clarified)
2 tablespoons flour
2 tablespoons dry bread crumbs
1 teaspoon Worcestershire sauce
salt and freshly ground black pepper

Sprinkle the venison cutlets with flour and pound them with the toothed side of a meat mallet. Turn the mallet and use the smooth side to pound the cutlets down to a thickness of ¼ inch. Set aside.

Cut the venison shoulder into chunks. Dice two strips of the bacon. Mix the venison shoulder and bacon and run it through a sausage mill, using a small wheel (⅛ to ³⁄₁₆ size). Set the ground meat aside.

Fry the other two strips of bacon in a large skillet. In the hot drippings sauté the onion and mushrooms until they start to brown. Stir in the ground meat and bread crumbs, along with a little salt and pepper. Spoon some of the stuffing onto each cutlet, roll, and secure with a toothpick.

Heat some butter in the skillet and sauté the venison rolls until browned on two sides, turning once. Add the wine, Worcestershire sauce, bouillon water, and meat stock. Bring to a boil, reduce the heat to very low, cover, and simmer until the venison is done and tender.

Serve hot with steamed cabbage sprinkled with crumbled bacon, boiled new potatoes sprinkled with a little dill weed, and plenty of crusty homemade bread..

Backstrap Chops with Red Wine

Note that no grease or breading is required for this recipe, making it a good choice for camp cooking, if you have the butter. If wild onions are available, try a few of these (½ cup) instead of the scallions.

backstrap chops for two
1 cup dry red wine
1 cup minced scallions, including part of the green tops
1 tablespoon butter
½ teaspoon dry mustard
salt and freshly ground black pepper to taste

Melt the butter in a saucepan. Sauté the scallions until tender and lightly browned. Then stir in the mustard and wine. Set the sauce aside and keep warm.

Heat a cast-iron skillet over hot coals, or on high heat if using a kitchen stove. Sear the chops for 2 minutes on each side. Carefully pour the sauce around the chops in the hot skillet. Add a little salt and pepper. Lower the heat and cook for 2 minutes.

Serve hot, topped with the pan juices, with wild rice and vegetables of your choice, along with some chewy French bread and the rest of the red wine.

Easy Big-Game Stir-fry

The accomplished stir-fry chef will mix his own sauces and marinades, but most of us can usually get by with a commercial mix. Almost always, soy sauce is the base for a good stir-fry sauce, flavored with ginger root and sake. Several good frozen stir-fry vegetable mixes are available in supermarkets and other outlets, such as wholesale clubs. I lean toward Oriental mixes, which usually contain snow peas. In addition to those packages with "stir-fry" printed on them, look over the dozens of other mixes available, such as the San Francisco blend. The meat? I like loin or tenderloin, but shoulder or rump can also be used, cut across the grain.

1 pound tender big-game meat
1 pound frozen stir-fry vegetables
stir-fry sauce
peanut oil
Mongolian Fire Oil (optional)
Asian sesame oil (optional)
cornstarch paste
rice (cooked separately)

Trim the meat and cut it into strips about ½ inch wide and 3 inches long. Put the meat into a nonmetallic container, pour in some some stir-fry sauce, toss to coat all sides, and marinate for several hours in a cool place. (How much sauce you use in the marinade isn't critical, but you don't need to completely cover the meat in liquid.)

When you are ready to cook, heat about 2 tablespoons of peanut oil in a cast-iron skillet. When the oil is very hot, quickly brown the meat in two or three batches, setting it aside to drain on a brown bag.

Add a little more oil if needed and stir-fry the vegetables for a few minutes. Put the meat back into the skillet, then add a little of the stir-fry sauce (or use the leftover marinade if you don't object to the blood), a few drops of Mongolian Fire Oil, and some sesame oil to taste. (Be sure to use the Oriental dark toasted-seed sesame oil used for flavoring, not the lighter sesame cooking oil.) Stir in the cornstarch paste, cover, and simmer for about 10 minutes, or until the vegetables are tender. Serve hot with rice.

Caribou Stroganoff

I was surprised to learn from Kira Petrovskaya's *Russian Cookbook* that the purists among Russian cooks would never add mushrooms or tomato paste to their Stroganoff. Although I like the mushrooms and think the tomato paste lends a nice color to the dish, I must confess that the true Russian way is very good, cooked as follows with caribou or tender venison of any sort. Bear, bison, or beef loin will work nicely.

1½ pounds caribou loin or tenderloin
1 cup meat stock or water
½ cup sour cream
1 medium to large onion, chopped
2 tablespoons whole-wheat flour
2 to 3 tablespoons clarified butter
1 strip of dry crust from a slice of pumpernickel bread
salt and pepper to taste
egg noodles, cooked separately

Cut the meat into thin strips. Heat most of the butter in a skillet. Roll the strips of meat in flour, then quickly brown them, a few at a time, in hot butter.

In a separate pan, sauté the chopped onion in a little butter. Add the onions to the meat pan along with the stock, bread crust, salt, and pepper. Simmer until the meat is very tender. Add the sour cream, then bring almost to a boil, stirring as you go to prevent the bottom from sticking. Add a little more stock or water if needed. Serve hot with noodles.

Variation: If you have some edible wild mushrooms, as I often have, slice and sauté them along with the onions and stir them into the meat. If the Russians don't like it, they can pick the mushroom slices out with their fork.

Squayrill Stoo

The little book *Bittle en' T'ing'*, or *Gullah Cooking with Maum Chrish'*, written by Virginia Mixson Geraty, is the best example of an authentic soul food cookbook that I have ever perused. The book contains only simple recipes, calling for a few basic ingredients.

Until modern times the Gullah lived for the most part off the land, in the Carolina and Georgia Low Country, using wild plants as well as garden fare and making do with a minimum of staples that could be stored for long periods of time. Since the Gullah ate lots of wild game and seafood, the book should be of interest to hunters, fishers, and camp cooks, who must often make do with limited "puhwishun" (as provisions are called in the Gullah tongue).

In this recipe, Maum says to skin the squirrel carefully and nail the hide up to dry for use as a collar. Give the tail to a young man to sport on his hat. Maum also says that one squirrel will make enough stew for four people, which indicates to me that she disremembered (as we say here in rural Florida) how small a squirrel is or that maybe she has been influenced by modern cookbook servings. I stick to one gray squirrel for the recipe below—then I eat the whole thing myself. Note that the fox squirrel, a species that is now protected in some areas, is much larger and will do for two. The authors and editors of many fish and game cookbooks don't seem to know the difference.

1 gray squirrel
1 medium-to-large onion, diced
flour
bacon drippings
salt and pepper

Sprinkle the squirrel pieces with salt and pepper. Shake them in a bag with flour. Heat the bacon drippings in a skillet and brown the squirrel pieces on both sides.

Remove the squirrel and sauté the onion until the edges start to brown. Put the squirrel pieces back into the skillet. Barely cover them with hot water. Bring to a light boil, reduce the heat, and simmer until the meat is tender and the gravy thick. Add more water and turn the squirrel from time to time if needed. (Be warned that an old boar squirrel with credentials will be very tough and needs long simmering.)

Serve with rice or biscuits.

Cross Creek Squirrel

Marjorie Kinnan Rawlings, author of *The Yearling*, lived on Cross Creek, which connects Orange Lake and Lake Lockloosa in central Florida. She cooked on a woodstove and made good use of butter from her cow, Dora, instead of using store-bought cooking oil or shortening. Miss Rawlings's squirrel recipe, which also works for rabbit, quail, and dove, can be made with ordinary supermarket butter. Be warned that an old squirrel is usually very tough and requires long, slow simmering; otherwise, you can't stick a fork in the gravy, as the saying goes. For that reason, it's best use young squirrels the first time you try this recipe.

young gray squirrels
butter
flour
salt and pepper to taste
boiling spring water

Skin, draw, and disjoint the squirrels, cutting them into 7 pieces as follows: 2 hind legs, saddle, rib section, 2 front legs, and head. Salt and pepper the pieces and roll them in flour, shaking off the excess.

Heat ¼ inch of butter in a deep skillet or Dutch oven. Brown the squirrel pieces on both sides. If you have to cook in more than one batch, add more butter as needed. Barely cover the squirrel pieces with boiling water. Cover the skillet tightly and simmer until the meat is very tender—an hour or more. Turn the pieces from time to time and add more water if needed to prevent scorching on the bottom.

Remove the squirrel pieces to a serving platter. Dissolve a little flour into the water and use it to thicken the gravy, stirring as you go and adding a little more salt and black pepper as needed. Serve the gravy over the squirrels, or put it into a gravy boat and serve it on the side. Squirrel gravy is great when spooned over rice or mashed potatoes.

Note: Be warned that some people in the Ozarks came down with something like mad cow disease, and all had been eating squirrel brains. Don't laugh. Squirrel heads were once a delicacy in rural areas, prized for their cheeks as well as the brains. They are still a good deal better than chicken heads. Still, I can't in good conscience recommend that you eat squirrel brains until the mad cow situation is better understood. So, forget the brains and content yourself with some good gnawing around the head. If you choose to live dangerously, however, or simply cannot resist squirrel brains, first gnaw the meat off the head, then cup it in your left hand and whop it with the back side of the spoon to crack the cranium so that you can get at the good stuff. It is not good manners, however, to suck the brains out at the table—at least not at my house. In camp, it's every man for himself.

Skillet Squirrel with Dried Morels

Any good mushroom will work with this recipe, but dried morels are hard to beat. Also try dried portabellos, oyster mushrooms, shiitakes, chanterelles, and so on. For cooking this dish to perfection, a heavy skillet is recommended. I use a cast-iron skillet, 10-inch diameter or larger.

2 gray squirrels cut into pieces
10 dried morels
cooking oil
flour
water
salt and pepper

Soak the dried mushrooms in water for 40 minutes or longer. Drain and slice the mushrooms, retaining the water. Salt and pepper the squirrel pieces, then shake them in a bag with a little flour.

Heat about ½ inch of oil in a skillet. Brown the squirrel pieces on both sides. It's best to have the oil quite hot so that the squirrel browns nicely and shows darker spots, almost to the burn stage, where it was in direct contact with the skillet. Drain the squirrel pieces.

Sauté the sliced morels in the skillet for a few minutes. Pour off most of the cooking oil. Using a wooden spoon, stir in a little flour. Cook for several minutes, stirring until you have a brown paste. Slowly stir in enough of the mushroom water to make a thin gravy, adding a little plain water if needed. Stir in some salt and pepper.

Fit the fried squirrel pieces in the skillet, cover tightly, and simmer (do not boil) on very low heat for about 1 hour, or until the squirrel is fork tender. Turn the squirrel pieces and add more water from time to time if needed. Serve hot, spooning the gravy over rice or biscuit halves. This dish is just too good.

Variation: Try cottontail rabbit or young muskrat instead of squirrel.

Aztec Rabbit

The Aztecs were fond of rabbits, and modern-day Mexicans of the central high-
lands share their enthusiasm in a special dish called mixiote, in which a rabbit
is cooked in a sack made from the inner membrane of the maguey plant. Re-
portedly this dish is so popular these days that it has curbed the production of
pulque, the national peasant beer made with the maguey (rather ironically, the
Aztecs had a rabbit god that presided over pulque, according to food guru Wa-
verley Root). Thankfully for the pulque trade, other rabbit dishes are also
cooked in Mexico, where several species (including the volcano rabbit) grow
wild. Often these recipes are quite long, but using prepared salsa will simplify
the process. Here's a recipe suitable for cooking two cottontails or one large
market rabbit or swamp rabbit (a hare) in a large skillet.

2 cottontails, dressed (or 1 market rabbit)
1 jar medium-hot tomato-based salsa (16-ounce size)
1 cup pulque or perhaps hard cider
1 cup chicken stock (or rabbit stock)
¼ cup ground walnuts or ground roasted peanuts
juice of ½ lemon or lime
2 tablespoons butter
2 tablespoons olive oil or bacon drippings
1 tablespoon chopped fresh cilantro
water as needed

After your wife dresses the rabbits, set aside the hind legs and saddles, telling
her to save the bony pieces (front legs, neck, and rib cage) for another recipe or
to make a stock to use herein. (To make a stock, cover the bony pieces with
water in a pot; add some chopped celery, carrot, and onion. Bring to a boil, reduce
the heat, cover, and simmer for about 2 or 3 hours, adding more water if needed.
Strain out the bones. Pull some of the easy meat off the front legs, mince it finely,
and add it to the liquid in the pot. Reduce the liquid over medium heat until you
have about 1 cup of stock. Substitute for the chicken stock in this recipe.)

Heat the butter and olive oil in a large skillet that has a lid. Brown the rabbit
pieces, turning a time or two. Set aside. Add the cilantro, salsa, stock, and
pulque to the skillet. Stir for a minute or so, then add the browned rabbit pieces.
Cover tightly and simmer for 3 hours; add more water from time to time as
needed and turn the pieces to keep them from burning.

Just before serving time, stir in the ground nuts and lemon juice. Simmer for 5 minutes. Serve hot, along with soft rolled tortillas for sopping. Feeds 2 to 4.

The Hunter's Responsibility

Many hunters find it convenient to haul their deer to a professional meat processor for butchering. There's nothing wrong with this practice, but the hunter should realize that putting prime venison on the table usually requires prompt field dressing. Omitting this step can be an irreversible mistake. Nothing in the butcher's bag of tricks can make neglected meat taste as good as it should. Venison gone bad won't even make acceptable sausage. In the kitchen, even the best cooks can't salvage gamy meat with secret marinades, fancy recipes, French sauces—or even country gravy.

What makes some venison taste gamy? Many people believe that blood is the culprit and will beseech the hunter to bleed the animal as soon as possible. They are probably wrong. Bleeding isn't necessary and may not help at all, except in cases where a queasy partaker has blood on the saddle and blood on the mind. For all practical purposes, you can forget about the blood during the field-dressing operation, unless you want to collect it for making French gravy. Trying to bleed the animal just makes a mess and takes up time that could be put to better use. While on the subject, however, I might add that merely slitting the animal's throat won't drain out much blood simply because the jugular connects only the heart and brain. To bleed properly (if you feel that you must), the animal should be hoisted up by its hind legs, or otherwise positioned with the head and shoulders downhill, and "stuck." That is, a stout knife blade is inserted through the breast and severs the aorta where it connects to the heart. (You'll know by the gush when you hit it.) But all this is simply not necessary. Besides, a good lung shot with modern ammo along with prompt field dressing does a pretty good job of bleeding deer.

Other people believe it's the intestines and bladders that cause the gamy taste. Although gut shots or improper field-dressing techniques can indeed cause some problems, the tainted meat is usually quite localized. As a rule, the guts, as such, really don't hurt anything—up to a point. (Of course, any discolored or "blood shot" meat should be cut out during the butchering phase.)

Yet, the innards should be removed from a dead animal as soon as possible—not for their own sake, but because of the heat they contain. That's right. Heat. It's as simple as that. This is especially true for large grazing animals, which tend to have lots of innards in terms of bulk, and for rabbits and hares. In short, removing the innards promptly after the kill takes away a good part of the animal's total heat and opens up the body cavity for ventilation and quick cooling. In addition to maintaining the quality of the meat, cooling discourages the growth of *E. coli* and perhaps other harmful bacteria that may be present.

There are several books and videos on how to field-dress a deer or other animal, but the process is really easy, especially for animals the size of whitetails and smaller. You simply roll the deer on its back, slit it open without cutting into the guts, turn it on its side, and dump the contents onto the ground. On a cool day you'll feel the heat rising from the pile of innards.

Of course, the hotter the day, the more urgent field dressing becomes. In the extremely cold weather of the far north, however, it may even be better to delay the field dressing a while. But usually quicker is better, and a cold day certainly doesn't give the hunter license to abuse the meat. Stuffing the deer into a closed car trunk or displaying it across the engine-heated hood of a pickup truck is a culinary sin.

Be warned, however, that prompt field dressing really can't salvage the meat from a deer, bear, or boar that has been chased all over the country with dogs before the kill. (Even a domestic hog so riled would taste gamy, and some farmers have been known to "scratch a hog down" with a corn-cob before dispatching it with a well-placed blow of a ball-peen hammer.) It also helps to drop the deer or other animal quickly with a well-placed shot.

Thankfully, prompt field dressing yields some ready meat for the camp cook. The tenderloin requires no aging, and the liver and other innards are best when fresh. The liver is especially perishable, whereas the heart and kidneys can be kept longer or frozen. Although fresh venison liver is one of my favorite wild-game foods (quickly sautéed with onions in some bacon drippings, along with a few good edible wild mushrooms, if available), some people simply don't want liver of any sort at any time—and especially not after field dressing the animal.

Note that some hunters and cooks mistake the venison loins for the tenderloins. The two loins run along the top of the backbone, one on either side. To get at them, the animal must be skinned, which often makes them inconvenient for deer camp cookery. The tenderloins, on the other hand, are smaller and run underneath the backbone, one on either side. They are clearly visible in the body cavity after the animal has been gutted, and they can be cut out easily with a pocket knife. I have known people who saved only the hind legs and loins from the deer, thereby throwing away the ribs, shoulders, and neck as well as the tenderloins—the filet mignon of the deer.

For a visual cross section of the loins and tenderloins, imagine two twin T-bone steaks or center-cut pork chops jutted back to back, with the bones fitted together at the saw line. The two larger top rounds will be the loins. The smaller bottom rounds, the tenderloins. Both are sometimes called "backstraps."

In closing, I might say to the hunter that giving gamy meat away, or expecting the butcher and cook to do the impossible, merely passes the buck. If the hunter shoots the animal, taking care of the meat is his responsibility. Or hers.

CHAPTER 6

Fish and Shellfish in the Skillet

Trout Hemingway, Reduced-Fat Catfish Fry, Lobster Norfolk, and A.D.'s Whole Scallop Fry, with Notes on Grouper Stacks

Most lean fish cook rather fast, about 10 minutes per inch of thickness, making the skillet a sensible way to prepare a mess for a few people. The skillet recipes below, both old and new, should whet the appetite for skillet fish and shellfish, with some emphasis on fried and sautéed fare, and a few other recipes appear here and there throughout the book. For blackened fish, see Chapter 12.

The Reduced-Fat Fish Fry

Fried catfish is a tradition in the South, and the dish is fast catching on in other parts of the country. While river-run channel cats are highly prized by many anglers and connoisseurs, most of the market fish are raised in ponds these days. In the rural South, small cats of about 7 inches in length are the favorites for frying, but fillets from larger fish are usually more popular in urban areas of the South as well as in other parts of the country. Either kind will do for frying, but steaks from very larger fish (cut across the backbone) are usually best when grilled or baked.

These days fried fish are frowned upon by many health-conscious people simply because they contain lots of fat. Yet, the fat absorbed by the fish during cooking can be reduced, as shown in the how-to details in this recipe. Even more important, the traditional menu can be altered to reduce the overall fat intake. The British fish 'n' chips, for example, is simply fried fish and french fries. The latter usually soak up more cooking oil than the fish, especially if cooked by the twice-fried gourmet recipes, in addition to the fat-producing carbohydrates in the potatoes. In the South, the traditional fish fry menu usually calls for hush puppies, which are nothing but fried corn pone, along with the fried fish and the twice-fried french fries. So, give some thought to the menu if you want to reduce the fat at a fish fry, or take a tip or two from the serving suggestions following this recipe, based on a contribution this ol' country boy made to a book called *One Fish, Two Fish, Crawfish, Bluefish: The Smithsonian Sustainable Seafood Cookbook*, published by the Smithsonian Institution in 2004, a work put together for the most part with recipes by famous chefs. (I knew that I, a self-proclaimed jackleg, would stick out like a sore thumb, but I did it anyhow, mostly because I felt that an unprissified recipe for farmed cats would leave more river-run fish for those of us in the know.) I have also published several versions of the recipe in other cookbooks and magazine pieces, and I can only assert that recent thinking makes it better or at least more practical for modern times.

catfish fillets or small whole fish
lots of peanut oil for deep frying
fine white cornmeal
salt and black pepper
Tabasco sauce (optional)

Rig for deep-frying in a cast-iron skillet, heating an inch of oil to 375°F. When the oil is almost hot enough, sprinkle the fish lightly on both sides with salt and pepper, along with a little Tabasco sauce, if wanted. Put about a cup of cornmeal into a small brown bag or a suitable container. (If you can't obtain fine stone-ground meal made from whole-kernel corn, use ordinary wheat flour.) Place a few fillets into the bag and shake it, coating all sides of the fish. Shake off the excess meal.

When the oil is hot, put a few fillets into the skillet. Do not overcrowd. Cook for a few minutes. The fillets are done when they float, but let them brown for another half minute or so. Carefully pick up the smallest fillet (larger ones take the longest to cook) with tongs and hold it over the skillet to drain some of the oil. Then place the fillet on a large brown bag. Drain the rest, one by one. Do not pile on or overlap the fillets, using more than one bag if necessary. (This brown bag will soak up a lot of grease from the fish. Several thicknesses of paper towel can be used, but brown bags really work better. Also, I usually serve the fish on the brown bag at informal feeds.) When the first batch of fish is done, let the oil heat back to 375°F and cook another batch, and so on. Serve hot with the serving suggestions below.

To recap: If you want to reduce the grease in the fried fish without losing flavor, be sure to follow the above steps closely, for these reasons: (1) A light coating of meal or flour will not soak up much oil, whereas some of the thick batters are grease traps. (2) Cooking the fish at a high temperature (and peanut oil can be heated quite hot before it starts smoking) tends to seal the surface of fish, keeping the pieces from soaking up oil. (3) Proper dripping over the skillet and draining on the brown bags will minimize the oil that you actually consume with the fish. This last step is more important than most people realize. Merely taking the fish up in a wire basket and piling them onto a serving platter can result in noticeably greasy fish—especially those on the bottom of the pile.

Another way to reduce the fat from a fish fry is to rethink the menu. I got onto this some time ago in north Florida, where many of the old Crackers serve fried fish for breakfast, along with grits and sliced tomatoes. Since I don't care much for grits, even when they are called polenta, I hit upon the idea of using instead whole-kernel hominy, which is available in canned form in most supermarkets, topped with tomato-based salsa. (Dried hominy can be obtained from Southwest markets, but it requires soaking and long cooking to make it tender.)

Each partaker puts a couple of fillets or small whole fish on half his plate, then spoons on some hominy and tops it with his choice of salsa (hot, medium, or mild). The plate is completed with sliced rounds of raw jicama, all garnished with a wedge or two of fresh lime. Lemon can be used, but the green lime makes a better color scheme with yellow hominy.

Trout Hemingway

I once started browsing about in *The Hemingway Cookbook* by Craig Boreth, enjoying Roast Duckling from the Harry's Bar, lunch with John Dos Passos, an Alice B. Toklas recipe or two (which seemed only tenuously connected to Ernest), Woodcock Flambé in Armagnac, and a few Algerian wines, which have an unusually high alcoholic content (owing to the hot summers, I learned). By chance I happened upon an early and less pretentious recipe for trout, first published by the young Hemingway in his outdoors column for the *Toronto Star*, long before he moved to France and fished the streams of Spain. He didn't specify the size of the trout, but they would have to be small enough to fit into a skillet. Granted, we can use a large skillet and cook the fish one or two at a time, but small trout in a 12-inch skillet work just right.

4 whole trout
8 strips bacon
1 cup cornmeal
1 cup Crisco

Build a good wood campfire, letting it burn down to coals. Pull out a sparse bed of coals and melt the Crisco in the skillet. Cook the bacon on medium heat until it is almost done but not yet brown. Dust the fish with cornmeal. Place the fish in the skillet and cook for 5 minutes. Turn and top each fish with 2 strips of the partly cooked bacon. Cook for about 10 minutes, or longer for larger trout. If cooked to perfection, Hemingway says, "The trout are crisp outside and firm and pink inside and the bacon is well done—but not too done."

Catalonian Fish with Garlic

Here's an old fisherman's dish from the Mediterranean coast of Spain. Like so
many other distinctive recipes, this one requires only a few ingredients. Don't
be put off by the amount of garlic, unless you simply can't stand the stuff, in
which case you probably wouldn't have gotten past the title of the recipe. The
trick to the recipe is to cook the garlic until it is "burnt" or, as modern chefs
say, well caramelized. I usually cook the dish in a cast-iron skillet large enough
to hold the fillets in a single layer, but other skillets, including an electric skillet,
will work fine. Any good, mild fish will work for this recipe. Try fillets of walleye
or black sea bass.

1 to 1½ pounds fish fillets
20 large cloves garlic
1 very large ripe tomato
olive oil
2 cups water
½ teaspoon sea salt

Peel the garlic cloves and slice them thinly lengthwise. Cut the tomato into
wedges (unpeeled) and remove the seeds. Then finely chop what's left of
the tomato.

Heat the oil in the skillet, add the garlic, and stir with a wooden spatula for
10 to 15 minutes, or until the garlic has turned dark brown. Add the chopped
tomatoes. Cook over low-to-medium heat, stirring with the wooden spatula, until
you have a rather dry paste. Stir in 2 cups of water, bring to a boil, and cook
until the sauce is reduced by half.

Sprinkle the fillets with sea salt, then place them in the skillet without overlapping them. On medium heat, cook the fillets from 3 to 5 minutes on each
side, turning only once, or until the flesh flakes easily when tested with a fork.
(The general rule applies: Cook for a total of 10 minutes per inch of thickness.)

Serve hot, spooning the sauce over each fillet. The sauce is also good
over rice.

Vietnamese Perch with Nuoc Cham

A condiment called nuoc cham (with some tricky accent marks) is essential to this dish, and Vietnamese fish sauce is essential to nuoc cham. Substitute Thai or Indonesian fish sauce if you must. In any case, nuoc cham is served with just about every meal in Vietnam, North or South, and is best prepared fresh for each meal, made with the aid of a mortar and pestle. It goes nicely with fried seafood. I normally use a fresh red cayenne pepper or Tabasco sauce for the recipe, but any fresh red chile will do.

As compared with the Chinese deep-fry, the Vietnamese use only a small amount of oil and do not often use a batter or flour coating. For this recipe, any good fish of about ½ pound can be used, preferably scaled. I list white perch, but also try bluegill or even crappie.

Nuoc Cham

2 tablespoons Vietnamese or Thai fish sauce
2 teaspoons light brown sugar
1 clove garlic
½ hot rod chile pepper (fresh) or to taste
⅛ lime (wedge)
water to taste

Seed and mince the pepper, carefully removing the inner pith as well as the seeds. Peel and mince the garlic. Put the pepper and garlic into a mortar, along with the sugar. Grind into a paste. Squeeze the juice of the lime into the mortar, then remove the lime pulp with a baby spoon or small knife and work it into the mixture with the pestle. Add the fish sauce, blending well. Slowly stir in the water to taste. (Note that the strength of the sauce depends on how much water you use; so, taste it as you go.) Pour the sauce into a small bowl and put it on the table, warning your guests that it is addictive.

The Fish

4 freshly caught white perch or similar fish
½ cup peanut oil

Scale and draw the fish, leaving the heads intact. Cut a shallow X on either side of each fish, just slitting the skin. Heat the oil in a skillet, getting it quite hot. Dry each fish with a paper towel and fry it quickly until both sides are nicely brown, turning once. Do not overcrowd the fish, frying in more than one batch if necessary.

Put the fish on a heated serving platter or directly onto each diner's plate. Spoon on a little sauce and serve with vegetables and breads of your choice. Remember that the Vietnamese eat lots of raw vegetables, so serve accordingly.

Skillet Fillets with Soy

This skillet dish can be made with any mild, white fish fillets of reasonable size. Bass, walleye, or channel catfish of about 1 pound each are ideal and will yield boneless and skinless fillets of about ¼ pound each. Allow two fillets per person. I like to cook the fillets in an electric skillet or a square cast-iron skillet.

4 fish fillets, boneless and skinned
1 medium onion, finely chopped
½ red bell pepper, seeded and finely chopped
½ green bell pepper, seeded and finely chopped
2 tablespoons soy sauce
2 tablespoons sake or dry vermouth
1 tablespoon peanut oil (maybe more)
½ tablespoon light brown sugar
salt and freshly ground black pepper to taste

Heat the oil in a large skillet. Sauté the fillets for 3 or 4 minutes, turning once. Carefully put the fillets onto a platter with the aid of spatulas.

Sauté the onion and peppers for 4 or 5 minutes, adding a little more oil if needed. Mix the soy sauce, sake or vermouth, and brown sugar. Stir the mixture into the skillet contents. Carefully place the fillets back into the skillet and spoon some of the sauce over the tops. Sprinkle lightly with freshly ground black pepper and more salt, if needed. (Remember that the soy sauce is quite salty.) Cover the skillet and simmer for about 10 minutes.

Serve the fillets and skillet sauce with rice, steamed vegetables or raw salad, and a crusty bread.

A Nassau Fish Steam

Here's an old Conch dish that has been traced back to the slaves that worked the cane fields in the Bahamas. There are many variations, such as this one adapted from *The Florida Cookbook*. Essentially, it's a method of steaming fish in a large covered skillet, and in the lower Keys it is called a "fish steam." I find that a 11- or 12-inch square electric skillet works great for these measures.

The recipe calls for cooked grits, which can be prepared easily from supermarket grits, following the directions on the package; for best results, however, the cooked grits should not contain lumps and should be cooked slowly and stirred with tender loving care. I might add that grits are often served with fried fish in Florida, especially at a Cracker breakfast.

The Old Sour asked for in the recipe is a popular condiment in the Florida Keys. It is made by mixing salt into freshly squeezed lime juice and fermenting for a couple of weeks. See the note below.

1½ pounds boneless fish fillets
3 cups hot grits (cooked separately)
2 medium Bermuda onions
2 Key or Persian limes
¼ cup butter
salt and pepper to taste
water as needed, about 2 cups
fresh lime wedges
hot pepper sauce such as Tabasco
Old Sour served in a cruet

Slice the onions and layer them in a large heated skillet. Cut the unpeeled limes into thin slices and layer over the onions. Add enough water to barely top the onions, cover the skillet, and simmer for 20 minutes.

Divide the fillets into at least four servings. Carefully place the fillets into the skillet, using tongs to pull some onions and lime slices over them. Add enough boiling water to almost cover the fish. Put a dab of butter over each fillet (saving about half the butter for the end) and sprinkle with salt (easy on the salt if you plan to use lots of Old Sour as a condiment) and freshly ground black pepper. Cover and simmer for 5 minutes, then spoon some of the pan juice over the fillets. Cover and simmer for another 4 or 5 minutes, or until the fish flakes easily when tested with a fork.

Serve in individual bowls or deep soup plates, with soup spoons. Put a large spoonful of grits in each bowl and top with a serving of fish, garnished with a little butter, onion, and lime slices. Each mouthful should contain some fish, some grits, and some broth. Have at hand plenty of lime wedges, Old Sour, and a perhaps a hot sauce such as Jamaican Pickapeppa or Dat'l Do-it (made from the Florida datil peppers), if wanted.

Note: To make a batch of Old Sour, sterilize a wide-mouth fruit jar (Mason jar) in boiling water. When the jar cools, add 2 cups freshly squeezed lime juice and 1 tablespoon sea salt. Shake to dissolve the salt. Put a clean square of cheesecloth over the top and tie with cotton twine or secure with a rubber band. Put the jar in a dark closet or cupboard for 6 to 8 weeks. Strain the juice with a piece of doubled cheesecloth and funnel it into sterilized serving bottles. (Old Conchs like to keep it in brown-colored Old Crow whiskey bottles.) Cork or cap the bottles and save until needed. Store in a dark place at room temperature. Old Sour is especially good at the raw bar or as a condiment for fish dishes and conch salad.

Panfish with Fiddleheads

Never miss the opportunity to gather a mess of fiddleheads from the ostrich fern (*Matteuccia struthioperis*) whenever you run across them in the forests or along a stream in the Northeast or find them for sale in a market. Fiddleheads are the tightly furled, unopened fronds of the very young ferns, picked as coin-shaped spirals an inch or so in diameter. They are best, I think, when first steamed or poached and then sautéed quickly in butter—which fits right in with fish cookery.

Some other fiddleheads are more or less edible and can be substituted with reasonable caution. Some authorities warn us, however, that some ferns produce fiddleheads that are carcinogenic. These suspects include the ubiquitous bracken fern, which is commonly eaten in Europe, Asia, New Zealand, Japan, and North America. In spite of the warnings of carcinogenic properties, I'll eat fiddleheads from any fern, including the bracken—but I'll do so in moderation. The small (less mature) fiddleheads are safer, and make the best eating.

The American Indians ate large quantities of raw fiddleheads before a hunt so that they would smell like the fern, a favorite deer food. The Indians also made bread from the roots of the bracken fern, and, in the Northwest they peeled the roots of the sword fern and baked them with salmon eggs in pits in the ground, much like the New England clambake.

panfish or fillets
fiddleheads
butter
all-purpose flour
salt and pepper
salted water

If you have fresh ferns, cut off the base and carefully remove the furry brown covering. Wash the fiddleheads and drop them into a pot of boiling salted water for 5 minutes. Drain.

Melt some butter in a skillet. Salt and pepper the trout to taste, dredge in flour, and sauté in butter until browned on both sides. Carefully remove the trout and drain on a heated platter. Add more butter to the skillet if needed and quickly sauté the fiddleheads.

Serve hot. Note that the fiddleheads can be boiled ahead of time. You can also use canned fiddleheads; these are precooked and should be drained, washed, and sautéed.

A.D.'s Cypress Trout

The ingredients list for this dish calls for a pound of stir-fry vegetables. For convenience, I often use a frozen mix, but most good, fresh vegetables will do. Try diced potatoes, Jerusalem artichokes, squash, onions, snow peas, cauliflower, and so on. As for the tsukeyaki (sukiyaki) sauce, I use chef Myron Becker's, available in some gourmet shops. If you can't find any such sauce locally, try mixing to taste a little soy sauce, sake, grated ginger, honey, a touch of lemon juice or lemon zest, and freshly ground black pepper. I designed this recipe to help cook the bowfin, also known as grinnel, mudfish, blackfish, cypress trout (my favorite), and countless unprintable names. Although acknowledged for its fighting ability on light tackle, the bowfin is generally regarded as a trash fish and presents the cook with a culinary challenge. If you can't catch a cypress trout, try using fillets from yellow bullheads or, better, a firm-fleshed fish such as sheepshead.

½ pound diced skinless fillets
olive oil
1 pound stir-fry vegetables
tsukeyaki (sukiyaki) sauce
rice (cooked separately)
cornstarch mixed with a little water

Cut the fillets into ½- to ¾-inch dice, cover with tsukeyaki sauce in a nonmetallic container, and marinate for 30 minutes.

Heat the olive oil in a cast-iron skillet. Drain the fish chunks and stir-fry on high heat for 2 minutes. Remove the fish with a slotted spoon or wire strainer. Drain.

Stir-fry the vegetables for a few minutes, adding a little more oil if needed. Put the fish back into the skillet, then add a little fresh tsukeyaki sauce. Cover and simmer for a few minutes, until all the vegetables are done.

Spoon some of the mix onto heated plates, along with some cooked rice. Quickly add some cornstarch paste to the remaining liquid in the skillet, stirring until the sauce thickens. Spoon a little sauce over the stir-fry and rice. Serve hot, along with crusty bread.

Salmon Patties

Salmon patties are made in a skillet with only a small amount of oil. The mixture should be rather thin so that it will flatten out easily. A salmon croquette, by comparison, is made with a stiffer mixture, coated with egg, dipped in bread crumbs, and fried in deep fat. It is easy to adapt this recipe to croquettes, if you so desire. (See also the next recipe.)

1 can salmon (24-ounce size)
3 medium to large chicken eggs
¼ cup clarified butter
1 tablespoon minced fresh parsley
salt and black pepper to taste

Drain and flake the salmon, retaining the juice from the can. Whisk the eggs lightly in a bowl. Add the salmon, parsley, salt, and black pepper. Mix well with your hands, and add a little of the reserved salmon juice, if needed. Heat the butter in a skillet. Shape the salmon mixture into patties about the size of your hand (sizing them so that only 2 or 3 fit into the skillet, unless you have to use a very large one).

Using a spatula, slip the patties into the hot butter and fry until golden brown on both sides, carefully turning once. Serve warm.

Note: Use vegetable oil if you prefer, and feel free to reduce the amount of the oil, using just enough to keep the patties from sticking.

Camp Croquettes

My mother often cooked salmon croquettes, but it never occurred to me to ask for her recipe. I'm certain that the ingredients list would call for chicken eggs, and I have watched her roll the formed croquettes in freshly crushed cracker crumbs. I haven't tried here to duplicate her results, but I have had occasion to cook my own creation in camp, where fresh eggs are likely to get broken.

The French definition for a croquette, on the other hand, calls for a cream sauce mixed in with the meat or fish, and I find that American canned cream soup works fine—just perfect for the camp cook. My recipe is simple enough, but cooking the croquettes to perfection requires some doing. I won't say the method requires skill, but a little practice will help. In short, if the mix is too mushy, the croquettes will flatten out in the skillet. If this happens, you can get yourself off the hook by calling the result salmon patties instead of croquettes. But the croquette-shaped ovals are more toothsome, being, if cooked perfectly in rather hot oil, crispy on the outside and creamy inside.

2 cans pink salmon (14¾-ounce size)
1 can cream of celery soup (10¾-ounce size)
1 sleeve saltines (about 40 crackers)
1 medium onion, minced
butter or olive oil
salt and pepper to taste

Drain the salmon and dump both cans into a mixing bowl. Stir in the soup and minced onions. Crush the saltines (while still in the sleeve if need be) into a fine meal and pour about three-quarters of this into the salmon bowl. Mix well, adding a little salt and black pepper.

Pour the rest of the cracker meal into a plate or onto a flat surface and spread it out. Shape the salmon mixture into croquettes about 1 inch in diameter and 3 inches long. As you go, carefully roll each croquette in cracker meal and line them up, side by side, on a plate or platter. (If you have a refrigerator or ice at hand, it's best to chill the croquettes for half an hour or so. This makes them easier to handle without tearing up or flattening out.)

Heat about 2 tablespoons of the butter or oil in a 10-inch skillet. Using a spatula, place several croquettes into the hot skillet one at a time; do not over-crowd. Cook them for several minutes, turning only once, until nicely browned on both sides. (Note that gently rolling the croquettes over, using the spatula and a spoon, is better than flipping them.) Serve hot with wild rice and vegetables of your choice.

This recipe will feed from 4 to 6 people. I recently tried the recipe with half measures, thinking that I could easily consume a can of a salmon. I had more croquettes than I wanted to eat at one sitting, but my dog Nosher was eager to help out. She now claims that these salmon croquettes are even better than my hush puppies.

Sautéed Bay Scallops

Small bay scallops, including the calico, are sweet and tender but firm if they are shucked and cooked shortly after capture. (The much larger sea scallops have a stronger flavor.) Market scallops are usually soaked in water, puffing them up. The bay scallops can be fried, broiled, or cooked in a number of ways, but they are really not large enough for kabobs. If you can't obtain fresh bay scallops, try the flash-frozen kind. In my neck of the woods, where the St. Joe Bay is home to an annual scallop festival, I can purchase flash-frozen eyes in 20-pound bags, with each one separate from the other so that I can take out what I want. My favorite way to cook them is hardly a recipe, but I'll list the ingredients anyhow just to make my point.

fresh bay scallops in the shell
salted butter

Shuck the scallops into a bowl, but do not wash off the saltwater. Heat some butter in a skillet and, on medium heat, sauté the scallops a few at a time. Drain on a brown paper bag.

If you are dining informally, serve the scallops on the brown bag, along with salad, steamed vegetables, and lots of chewy French bread. Enjoy. Go and catch some more scallops! If you catch only a few, however, and need to stretch the menu while experiencing a rather daring new culinary adventure, see the following recipe.

A.D.'s Whole Scallop Fry

Our thinking about scallops has been greatly influenced by what's available in our commercial markets, on restaurant menus, and in recipes, which invariably limit the choice to the bay (or calico) and sea scallops that grow along the Eastern Seaboard, ignoring West Coast species.

I suppose that properly equipped frogmen can dive for their own sea scallops, but most of the recreational scalloping is for the small bay or calico species. These can sometimes be taken in very shallow water, often around eelgrass beds, by wading. The scallops can be caught with a small net, or simply picked up by hand. A snorkel, mask, and swim fins may come in handy, and sometimes diving a few feet will be quite productive. Of course, conditions vary from one good scalloping spot to another, so it's always best to check with local sportsmen and tackle shops before wading in. Note also that scalloping is highly regulated in most areas these days, with seasons and bag limits. From time to time certain waters may be closed owing to low reproduction rates, which can swing wildly from one season to the next—or because contamination of some sort makes the shellfish unsafe for human consumption.

Happily, frozen farmed scallops are now available, and it's even possible these days for landlubbers to purchase live (unshucked) farmed scallops with overnight delivery. For openers, check with *www.farm-2-market.com*—or roll your trousers and go Googling. Oh, 'tis a brave new world for culinary sports, and now is the time to take a hard look at eating the whole scallop, not just the white adductor muscle, which is the only part that is commonly eaten in America. In other parts of the world the whole scallop is often consumed, but those books and magazine articles that mention eating the whole thing are a little short on details. I know why. Anyone who has shucked a bay scallop and examined the insides up close will not be too enthusiastic about eating what he sees. Don't be put off. Just remember that from this ugly mess arose Aphrodite, and try this method of making the whole scallop prettier to see and easier to swallow. The trick is to fry the scallop in the half shell, following a method sometimes used in Alaska to fry butter clams.

whole bay scallops, freshly gathered
flour, cracker crumbs, or finely ground white cornmeal
peanut oil for frying

Heat about an inch of peanut oil in a deep skillet. While the oil is heating, partly shuck some of the scallops, removing the top part of the shell but leaving the bottom part attached by the adductor muscle. Do not clean out the insides or spill out the juice.

Spread some flour or other breading onto a plate. Going one by one, set the scallop into the flour shell-side down. Sprinkle some of the flour generously onto the open scallop. Carefully dump out the excess flour. (This will leave some breading mixed with the natural juices of the scallop. Be warned that hot grease and water mix violently, so make sure all the juice is absorbed and won't spill out into the skillet.) Repeat until you have enough breaded scallops to fit loosely into the skillet.

When the oil is hot, carefully set each scallop into the skillet shell-side down. (I use a slotted kitchen spoon, with scalloped tongs at hand if needed.) Fry for a couple of minutes, until the inside of the scallop shrinks a little. Turn the scallops over, meat-side down now, and fry two or three minutes, or until nicely browned. Remove the scallops, draining with a slotted spoon, and place them shell-side down on a serving platter or plate. These make an attractive presentation.

To eat, scoop out the scallop with a regular table spoon, dislodging the adductor muscle and good stuff as you go. All the innards will have pulled into a solid mass, and the whole stays together for a one-bite experience. The breading, soaked with scallop juice and fried, makes for a flavorful crunch. The sensation is not unlike eating a fried oyster, with a crusty outside and a juicy inside—but with the added chewiness of the adductor muscle. It's a toothsome morsel.

Note that this technique can also be used on some clams as well as small mussels or even well-scrubbed small oysters.

Finger-Licking Shrimp

Here's one of my favorite ways to cook shrimp. I like to cook it with a season-ing mix called lemon pepper, available on the spice rack of any supermarket (but I also like to make my own with dried lemon zest, finely ground sea salt, and black pepper). In recent times, a number of seasonings have become available, often in the name of regions, or ethnic or national cuisines. For this recipe, a salt-based seasoning works best. Thus, it's easy to vary your season-ing to suit the theme of the rest of the feast.

In any case, the recipe works best with very fresh heads-on shrimp, which are available in some areas, usually near the coast. Beheaded but unpeeled shrimp also work but are not ideal. The idea is for each diner to shuck his own shrimp at his plate, thereby getting some of the oil and seasonings on his fin-gers. (Anyone who worries about deveining the shrimp won't get his fair share at my table, as the pile will quickly diminish.) I like a large skillet for these, 12- or 14-inch, if several people are to partake.

very fresh shrimp, heads on, medium to large size
olive oil
lemon pepper, Cajun dust, or similar shake-on seasoning
chewy French bread

Wash and drain the shrimp, but do not peel them. Heat half an inch of oil in a large skillet. Cooking in two or more batches if necessary, sauté the shrimp in a single layer for 2 or 3 minutes, turning once. (Very large shrimp may require longer cooking—but not much. As a rule, the shrimp are ready when they turn pink. If they are cooked too long, they will be a little tough and, even more impor-tant, the meat will tend to stick to the shell, making them hard to shuck. A prop-erly cooked shrimp should peel very easily and burst with flavor in the mouth.)

When done, remove the shrimp with a strainer or large slotted spoon and drain on a brown bag. Sprinkle with lemon pepper, or seasoning salt of your choice. Use the brown bag for serving, putting it in the middle of the table, along with a large serving spoon, and letting each partaker get his own. When shuck-ing the shrimp, the fingers become coated with the oil and seasoning, which ex-plains the finger-licking part of the recipe. Serve with a crusty French bread and plenty of salad, preferably with lots of chopped garden-fresh tomatoes in the green stuff.

Skillet Shrimp with Sweet Peppers

Here's an old recipe from coastal Georgia and the Low Country in South Carolina, where shrimp like to run up the tidal creeks. Small or medium shrimp work best, boiled in salted water for only 2 or 3 minutes, until they are nicely pink. Cooking the shrimp longer makes them tough and difficult to peel. An electric skillet works just fine for this recipe.

2 cups peeled boiled shrimp
2 cups chopped tomato
2 bell peppers seeded and cut into strips
6 slices of bacon
2 cloves garlic, minced
½ teaspoon red pepper flakes
salt and freshly ground black pepper to taste
white rice (precooked)

In a large skillet fry the bacon until it is crisp. Remove the bacon and set aside, leaving the drippings in the skillet. Add the bell pepper strips and cook for a few minutes, stirring a time or two. Add the garlic, chopped tomato, and red pepper flakes. Cover and cook very slowly for about half an hour, stirring frequently. Add a little water if needed.

Add the shrimp along with some salt and freshly ground black pepper. Cook for about 5 minutes. Serve on a bed of rice, with a green salad topped with crumbled bacon on the side.

Lobster Norfolk

This old recipe from the Chesapeake Bay area can also be cooked with lump crabmeat. Be sure to use regular butter, not unsalted. I allow half a pound of meat per person. That's quite a bit, but it's so good that you'll be looking for seconds. Try this one with spiny lobster (sometimes called crawfish in Florida) or the smaller bulldozers (shovel lobsters).

1 pound lobster meat, uncooked
1 cup butter

Warm two serving ramekins in an oven on low heat. Cut the lobster meat into bite-sized servings. Melt the butter in a cast-iron skillet. Add the lobster meat and increase the heat to high. Cook for 3 or 4 minutes, stirring with a wooden spoon. Reduce the heat to low and cook for 4 or 5 minutes, stirring and tilting the skillet in a circular motion.

Spoon the lobster into the warmed ramekins and pour the butter left in the skillet equally over each serving. Serve in the ramekins, along with plenty of chewy bread and lots of pretty salad.

Easy Camp Chowder

New Englanders claim that good fish chowder can't be made without chowder crackers, a regional staple that no doubt evolved from the old sailor's hardtack. Well, here's a camp chowder that may violate New England sensibilities—but taste it before you start writing nasty letters and accuse me of trying to start the Civil War again.

½ to 1 pound of fish fillets
1 can cream of clam chowder (10¾ ounce size)
1 pound small red potatoes, sliced
1 medium to large onion, chopped
several strips of salt pork (or bacon if need be)
salt and freshly ground black pepper
oyster crackers, saltines, or chewy French bread

Dice the salt pork and fry it in a 12-inch skillet until the oil is cooked out. Drain the cracklings and set aside. In the drippings, sauté the onion for a few minutes, stirring as you go. Layer on the sliced potatoes and add the fish chunks. Sprinkle lightly with salt and pepper. Dump in the can of clam chowder. Rinse out the can with water, pouring the contents into the skillet to add more moisture. Cook on reduced heat for about 12 minutes. Don't stir while cooking, but check with a spoon to make sure the bottom isn't about to scorch.

If all goes well, the chowder can be removed in layers, almost like a slice of pie. If you want it more soupy, simply add a little water and serve along with the French bread for sopping, or serve topped with either oyster crackers or saltines for crunch. In either case, sprinkle each bowl of the finished chowder with the cracklings before digging in.

Fried Panfish Roe

I usually cook this recipe whenever I find roe in fish destined for the skillet or deep fryer. In other words, I cook and serve the roe along with the fish. (Larger roe, such as that of mullet, can also be fried, but it tends to be rather dry and pops dangerously in hot oil.)

bluegill or shellcracker roe
peanut oil
stone-ground white cornmeal or white flour
fine salt

Dress the bluegill carefully, trying to avoid cutting into the roe sacs. Keep the sacs intact (joined). Rig for deep-frying at 370°F. Salt the roe to taste and shake in a bag with the cornmeal. Stand back in case of oil spatters and fry the roe for 3 or 4 minutes, until lightly browned. Serve along with fried panfish.

Skillet Softcraws

Most anglers know that soft-shelled crawfish make better live bait than hard-craws. Few realize, however, that softcraws can also be much better additions to the camp skillet, and can, in fact, save the day.

The problem with crawfish cookery in general is that the tail end is small in relation to the head, and the delicious white meat gets even smaller when you shuck it out for frying. If the crawfish are small to start with (and few of the 200 species that grow around the country will measure up to the Louisiana reds), then Livingston's Law of Futile Foraging sets in. Roughly stated: the energy expended in catching, dressing, cooking, and eating the prey is more than that derived from its consumption.

Still, in Mid-America every country boy's dream is to get up enough crawfish to feed the whole family. A culinary breakthrough down in Cajun country can make this task much easier. If you are lucky enough to catch a softcraw, you can fry and eat the whole thing—almost. This shortens the preparation time, simplifies the eating, and reduces the energy expended on catching the food, simply because a few softcraws can go a long way.

Like crabs, crawfish molt from time to time, usually in spring or summer. After shedding the old shell, the crawfish quickly grows a new one, drawing from two balls of calcium that have been built up inside its head. These look like pearly BB's. Although the new shell grows surprisingly fast, the molting crawfish is left with a soft shell for a few hours. There will be an optimum stage of softness for eating purposes, but the hungry sportsman probably won't even notice a little crunch.

The idea of eating soft-shelled crustaceans whole is really not new. Along the East Coast and the Gulf of Mexico, old salts and adventurous vacationers have long since taken advantage of the soft-shelled blue crabs. At market these were expensive and not always available. In time commercial holding tanks were developed, enabling the crabber to have more control over nature. At present, both fried and broiled soft-shells are not unusual items on the menu of coastal eating houses.

The holding-tank idea can also be applied to crawfish. The process is relatively new, however, and how widely available softcraws become remains to be seen. There are marketing problems even with hard crawfish, which are often precooked before they reach the consumer. In any case, Googling "crawfish cookery" on the Internet will keep you up to date.

Fortunately, the sportsman and wild foods forager doesn't have to wait for a softcraw market to develop. Just about every lake, pond, stream, and wet-water ditch in the country will hold plenty of live crawfish, free for the taking.

Further, the smaller species of crawfish may be even better, culinarily speaking, than the larger commercial varieties. A small softcraw properly fried makes a nice bite, at once crispy and succulent.

You can cook this recipe with all softcraws, if you have them, or you can fill in with peeled tails from hardcraws. This approach will enable the forager to use a mixed bag. If you can't get up a combined mess of soft- and hardcraws, add a few small fish to fill in. Hornyheads or any perch will do. If gashed and crisply fried, these can be eaten bones and all.

2 dozen live soft-shelled crawfish or substitutes
peanut oil for deep frying
2 chicken eggs whisked with a little milk
flour
fine bread crumbs
salt and cayenne to taste

To prepare the live softcraws for frying, rinse them and snip off the front part of the head, cutting in right behind the eyes with kitchen shears. Squeeze the head a little and watch for the balls of calcium to come out of the cut. Remove these and discard the pointed part of the head. Be warned that both calcium balls should be accounted for; these things are as hard as steel bird shot and simply must be removed, lest one of your guests break a tooth at the table.

To proceed, heat 3 or 4 inches of peanut oil to 350° or 375°F in a suitable pot or fish fryer. Put the flour into a small brown bag, along with some salt and cayenne pepper. Put the bread crumbs into a separate bag. Dip the crawfish one at a time in the whisked egg, drop it into the flour bag, and shake it. Dip the dusted crawfish in the egg again, then shake in the bread crumbs. Fry the breaded crawfish, a few at a time, for 2 or 3 minutes, or until golden brown. Drain on brown bags. Serve hot.

Grouper Stacks

This sandwich has become a favorite lunch in family eateries around the Gulf of Mexico. A plump fillet about an inch thick and large enough to stick out over the bread is the key to the stack. Bread the grouper fillets and fry until golden brown and crispy, but soft and moist inside. Slather the insides of two slices of thick sandwich bread with mayonnaise, tartar sauce, or some such "twangy" white spread. Sandwich with a fried fillet, followed by a slice of red-ripe tomato, salt, pepper, and a little lettuce, either sliced or shredded. A thin slice of mild onion or a few onion rings can also be added, if wanted. Serve with twice-fried shoestring potatoes and dill pickle spear on the side. A wedge of lemon adds a little color.

Note: Many commercial eateries give the customer the choice of fried, grilled, or blackened fillets for building a grouper stack. I suspect that many of the "grilled" fillets are simply sautéed, but some might well be cooked over hot coals. In any case, I prefer to have mine crisply fried (unless I am doing the grilling over real coals) instead of soggy—but I certainly won't turn down any well-laid grouper stack. Note also that most mild fish with flaky white meat can be used in this recipe. Fillets of black bass are perfect.

Walleye Fillets with Verjuice

The author of a Texas cookbook wrote that she liked to gather wild grapes along the streams in the spring of the year. Well, the wild grapes in my neck of the woods get ripe in August and September, and possibly October, instead of in the spring. But you don't have to wait until the grapes are fully ripe to enjoy them. Juice from large green immature grapes (or sour grapes) was once very popular as a cooking ingredient, used pretty much like lemon juice or vinegar. Called verjuice, it was especially popular in Europe during the Middle Ages and in ancient Egypt, where it was used with fish. Verjuice is still used in the Caucasus, and I have even seen the ingredient listed a time or two in modern American recipes. You too can use it, in camp or at home.

Although the recipe below calls for walleye fillets, any good white-fleshed fish can be used. Try small flounder or white perch or tilapia.

walleye fillets
butter
verjuice
flour
salt and pepper

Salt and pepper the fillets to taste, then dust them lightly with flour. Heat the butter in a skillet and sauté the fillets, browning nicely on both sides. Remove the fillets with a spatula, placing them on a heated serving platter or onto plates. Add the verjuice to the skillet, along with more butter if needed. Cook and stir constantly until the sauce thickens a little. Pour the sauce over the fish and serve hot.

Sumac Trout

I claim bragging rights to this recipe, which I published in a previous book. Try it the next time you see bunches of sumac berries growing along a stream or shoreline. That's right. Sumac. All of the American sumacs with red berries (genus *Rhus*) can be used; these include staghorn sumac, scarlet sumac, squawbush, smooth sumac, and others. The berries are covered with tiny hairs, which in turn are coated with a substance called malic acid. This stuff has a pleasing, tart flavor. In the Middle East, sumac berries are used to make a spice, and ancient recipes from Apicus (the Roman culinary sport) call for Syrian sumac.

A pleasing drink, sometimes called Indian lemonade, can be made from the sumac berries and a little sugar. Usually, the drink is made by sloshing some berries around in cold water. The berries don't have to be crushed, since most of the flavor is on the tiny hairs that grow on the surface. The liquid is then strained through a double thickness of cloth to get rid of the spent berries and the fine hairs that shed off. (Note that washing the berries in the stream will rob them of flavor; note also that a strong rain can wash the flavor from the berries, so that it's best to get them during dry weather.)

In addition to making Indian lemonade, the early American settlers used a sumac infusion as a substitute for lemon juice, which is what gave me the idea for this recipe. To make what I call sumac concentrate, boil some of the juice (unsweetened) until it is reduced enough to suit your taste.

If you like the flavor of sumac, remember that the berries grow in large bunches and are very easy to gather. So, fill your canoe before the rains come. The berries can be stored in a dry place for winter use, or you can freeze the juice. Make a little extra concentrate and try it in recipes that call for lemon juice, just as the early American settlers did. Then you can smile the next time you price a lemon in the supermarket.

1 or 2 small trout, less than 1 pound
2 or 3 tablespoons butter
flour
sumac concentrate
salt to taste

Dress the trout with or without heads, depending on the relative size of your skillet, and sprinkle inside and out with salt. Dust the trout lightly with flour. Melt the butter in the skillet. Sauté the trout until done on both sides, turning once. Remove the trout to drain. Add a little sumac concentrate to the skillet, stirring and shaking the pan for a few minutes. Taste and add more sumac, or more butter, if needed. Pour the sauce over the trout and eat hot.

CHAPTER 7

Exotic Meats

**Newfie Cod Tongues, Fried Soft-Shell Turtle,
A.D.'s Cricket Crisps, Chicken-Fried Gator,
and Other Culinary Treats**

Internet marketing, flash-freezing techniques, and overnight shipping have made it a brave new world for culinary sports across the land. Slowly, American tastes are evolving, helping us appreciate the incredibly wide range of foods eaten around the world and now available to the modern epicure. A short chapter in a short book like this can't possibly do justice to this new cookery, but maybe the few recipes below will inspire us to go Googling for new tastes and exotic flavors. More important, perhaps the new cuisine and fusion cookery will cause us to take a closer look at what is available in our own backyards or at the local bait shop.

Chicken-Fried Gator

Alligators always get attention, whether on TV, golf courses, in the wild, or, these days, on the menu of some upscale restaurants from Dallas to New York City. They have always been welcome table fare for old Florida Crackers and Louisiana swamp dwellers. Even when on the endangered species list a few years back, gators were farm raised for profit and were poached illegally for hides and meat. These days gators are legal game in some areas, "harvested" by state-run lottery permit and strict regulations. Many of the regular hunters, at least here in Florida, recoup part or all of the fees and expenses of the hunt by selling the hides. Some even show a good profit, in spite of high permit fees.

The hunts are all right, I guess, but legally you can't simply go out and shoot a gator the way you would a deer or a turkey. The many rules and regulations for the hunts are available on the Internet, along with butchering procedure, hide care, outfitters, guides, and so on. For openers, try *www.wildflorida.org/gators/public.htm*, or perhaps search for alligator meat on *google.com*. If your main interest in the gator is culinary, you may decide to purchase some meat from one of the many suppliers, or from a professional hunter who "rescues" the "nuisance" gators in several states. Names and addresses are also available on the Internet.

In any case, remember that most of the gator meat on the market is from large specimens, partly because the hide is more valuable than the meat. Large gators tend to be tough. In many cases, the meat sold on the market has been "cubed." That is, it has been tenderized with a machine, making it similar to the cubed beef and pork sold at supermarkets. The same effect can be achieved by pounding the meat with the cubing side of a hand-held meat mallet. If you want the meat at its best, catch yourself a yearling of 4 or 5 feet—and field-dress it as soon as practical.

In any case, here's a recipe that works best with market meat that has been run through a meat-tenderizing machine. If you butcher your own gator, use a meat mallet to flatten the meat to about ⅜ inch thickness. Servings? I allow at least half a pound of gator per person. More is better, within reason. The measures below can be modified to suit your needs or your appetite.

2 pounds cubed gator
juice of two lemons (plus one for Plan B, if needed)
2 cups all-purpose flour
1 medium onion, minced

¼ cup half-and-half

1 tablespoon salt

2 teaspoons finely ground black pepper

1 teaspoon cayenne

peanut oil

Put the meat into a plastic zip bag and add the lemon juice, turning about to coat all sides. Refrigerate for several hours. When you are ready to cook, drain the meat and heat ½ inch of peanut oil in a cast-iron skillet. Mix the salt, black pepper, and cayenne into the flour and put it into a medium-sized brown bag. Shake the meat, a few pieces at a time, in the bag and set aside, retaining the seasoned flour.

Fry the meat a few pieces at a time on high heat for a couple of minutes on each side, until nicely browned. Drain the meat on a brown bag. Take a bite. If it is too tough to chew, resort to Plan B below. If it is tender, proceed as follows: Pour off most of the skillet oil, leaving about 1½ tablespoons. Sauté the minced onion. Sprinkle a little of the reserved flour into the skillet, stirring as your go, until you have a light roux. Slowly stir in the half-and-half until the gravy is as thin as you like it.

Serve the steaks on individual plates, topping each one with some of the gravy, along with rice and vegetables of your choice. Swamp cabbage (heart of palm) always goes nicely with gator.

Plan B: If the meat is too tough to chew after frying, set it aside and pour most of the grease out of the skillet. Put the browned meat back into the skillet and sprinkle with a little of the reserved flour. Add the juice of another lemon, along with enough water to cover the meat. Bring to a boil, reduce the heat to very low, cover tightly, and simmer for two hours or longer—until the meat is tender. Stir and add more water as needed.

Island Frogs

The legs of crapauds, also known as mountain chickens, the large frogs found in Dominica and Montserrat, are considered to be gourmet fare in island circles. The recipe also works nicely for the legs of large stateside bullfrogs. The marinade helps the texture of the meat in addition to adding flavor.

2 pounds large frog legs
1 medium onion, grated
3 cloves garlic, crushed
cooking oil
flour
1 tablespoon red wine vinegar
1 tablespoon rum
1 teaspoon salt
½ teaspoon white pepper
½ teaspoon freshly ground allspice
lime wedges for garnish

Mix the wine vinegar, rum, onion, garlic, allspice, salt, and white pepper in a non-metallic container. Add the frog legs, toss about to coat all sides, and marinate for an hour or so, turning from time to time.

When you are ready to cook, heat the oil in a skillet. Drain the frog legs and shake them in a bag of flour. Shake off the excess flour, then fry the frog legs a few at a time in the skillet for about 5 minutes on each side, turning once. Brown nicely but do not overcook. Drain the frog legs on a brown bag and serve hot, along with lime wedges.

Frogs Sturdivant

Large American bullfrog legs tend to be a little stringy when fried like chicken. In this regard, legs from the smaller leopard frogs, once harvested commercially in the Florida Everglades, are better than big ol' speckled-belly river swamp bulls. Also note that commercial frogs, some pond-raised in Asia, are available in several sizes. Medium or small are better for frying, although some people think that large is better.

The whole frog can also be cooked, and, I'll submit, the front legs are a little better in that they have a shorter muscle fiber. In spite of numerous "eye-witnesses," dead frogs of any size don't jump out of the skillet. In any case, here is a recipe, adapted from *Game Cookery* by E.N. and Edith Sturdivant, that tames frog legs considerably and improves the texture on the big ones. Note that the frog legs are lightly parboiled before they hit the hot skillet.

8 pairs frog legs
½ cup lemon juice
1 chicken egg
cracker crumbs
salt and freshly ground black pepper to taste
cooking oil
water for poaching

Bring some water to a boil and add the lemon juice and a little salt. Simmer the frog legs for 2 minutes. Drain.

Beat the chicken egg in a bowl and place some cracker crumbs in a plate. Sprinkle the legs with salt and pepper, dip them one at a time in the egg, and roll them in the cracker crumbs. Heat about an inch of oil in a skillet and fry about half the legs until golden brown, usually from 3 to 5 minutes, depending on the size of the legs. Drain the legs on a brown bag and cook the rest.

Serve hot, along with rice, a green vegetable, and hot biscuits.

Note: For very large legs from those old speckled-belly frogs, you may want to marinate in lemon juice before parboiling.

Fried Soft-Shell Turtle

A young soft-shell, about the size of a dinner plate, is tender and succulent and fries as nicely as a yearling squirrel. It's best to cook it quickly in hot grease. I have read that the outer edge of the soft-shell turtle is edible, provided that it is simmered until tender. Personally, I don't care for it and consider its culinary quality, like that of the beaver tail, to be a campfire joke. Freshwater soft-shell turtles can be caught from lakes and streams, and the large Florida soft-shells can be purchased from specialty meat shops.

young soft-shell turtles
peanut oil for deep frying
flour
salt and pepper
water or stock (for gravy)

Dress and disjoint the turtles, salt and pepper the pieces, and shake in a bag with flour. Rig for deep-frying in a stove-top Dutch oven or other suitable pot. Fry the turtle a few pieces at the time until they are nicely browned. Drain the pieces on a brown bag.

If you want gravy, pour most of the oil out of the Dutch oven. Add a little flour, stirring with a wooden spoon. Slowly add some water or stock, stirring as you go, until you have a thick gravy. Serve the turtle hot, spooning the gravy over rice, mashed potatoes, or biscuit halves.

Note: If the turtle is a little tough for your liking, put the pieces into the gravy, cover, and simmer on very low heat until tender, adding a little water from time to time if needed, as in Plan B for Chicken-Fried Gator.

Turtle Stew with Acorn Gravy

Some of the best eating often comes from a sparse cupboard supplemented with plenty of good wild foods. Once, while living in the country, I needed to feed a couple of hungry college boys on short notice. Looking around in the freezer, I found a piece of snapping turtle that I had been saving—actually, it was from a large turtle my younger son had caught from our cypress pond. Tough, yes, I knew it would be tough, partly because we had already eaten about 10 pounds of the meat. The remaining pound or two was from a leg quarter—one of the toughest parts. Consequently, I knew that long cooking would be in order.

In the freezer I found a package of tough oyster mushrooms that I had gathered one morning from the trunk of an ancient oak near the cypress pond. These were the last of about 2 gallons of beautiful mushrooms, and I knew from experience that they hold up to long cooking. In the freezer I also found a few pods of okra that I had been saving for a gumbo, along with a small package of frozen wild onions with part of the green tops. In the cupboard was a can of tomatoes. We had plenty of rice.

My first thoughts pointed toward a turtle-and-okra gumbo, but I changed my mind while considering a pile of sweet live oak acorns on my countertop. A turtle-and-acorn stew with tomato and wild onions would be in order (real Indian chow) served up over a bed of steamed rice. Vegetables? Across the fence from the pond grew a field of soybeans. The stalks were planted thick, and each stalk was loaded with pods. These were still in the green stage, and I had always wanted to try them cooked like green field peas—one of my favorite Southern dishes. I had previously shelled a few pods and and put the green beans into a vegetable soup. The okra pods could be cooked right in with the soybeans, a combination that was at one time quite popular in the rural South.

Some of the soybeans were quite mature and had to be cooked for about 40 minutes. They were delicious and held their texture and green color better than field peas. Since America grows countless tons of soybeans each year, I don't understand why we don't eat more of them while they are still green. In addition to being very good, they are loaded with protein. These are merely simmered for 30 or 40 minutes in water, preferably seasoned with a little salt pork or ham hock.

Anyhow, here's the recipe for the turtle stew with acorn gravy. I published a version of the recipe in my column for *Gray's Sporting Journal*. Since then I have doubled the measure of mushrooms.

1 pound turtle meat

¼ to ½ pound oyster mushrooms

1 can tomatoes (14½-ounce size)

acorn meal

cooking oil

wild onions with part of green tops

water

salt and freshly ground black pepper

rice (cooked separately)

Cut the turtle meat into small cubes. (The meat can be stringy, so small pieces are easier to eat.) Heat a little cooking oil in a large skillet, then brown the turtle meat and the wild onions. Add the can of tomatoes, along with the liquid from the can, and the oyster mushrooms. (The mushrooms should be cut into slices.) Add about two tomato cans of water. Bring to a boil, reduce the heat, cover tightly, and simmer for 2 or 3 hours. Add more water from time to time as needed. It's best to barely simmer the meat instead of boiling it.

When the meat is very tender, add some salt and freshly ground black pepper. Sprinkle on a little acorn meal, stirring and cooking as you go, until you have a gravy. I don't use exact measurements, but about a tablespoon of acorn meal will be about right. Add more water if needed.

Cook and stir, cook and stir, until the dish acquires a deep, dark brown color. (Acorn meal tends to turn quite dark when cooked.) The acorns add to the flavor, and the color makes the stew go nicely over a bed of white rice. Serve with cooked soybeans or other vegetables and a crusty bread. Sop the gravy.

Note: Substitute mushrooms of your choice for the oyster mushrooms, but remember that some of these would have to be cooked for the whole time. Also, sundried tomatoes work nicely in this recipe.

Warning: Make sure that you have sweet acorns for this recipe. Bitter acorns, usually of a black oak variety, require special handling and much soaking in water to get out the bitter tannin. When I first published this recipe in *Gray's Sporting Journal*, a school teacher from Georgia sent me an acorn recipe book put together by her students. One recipe for acorn soup called for 2 gallons of macaroni and 1 acorn. Clearly, the boy got hold of a bitter acorn for testing purposes.

Higado de Tortuga

To Peru we go. The whole country has wonderful food, including about fifty kinds of potato, one of which is actually freeze-dried in the high Andes by an ancient procedure. The coastal areas have seafood in great plenty and the people in the mountains still eat alpaca and guinea pigs, but my favorite recipes come from the east of the Andes—a vast Amazonian expanse, which the Spanish conquistadors failed to conquer. In addition to the regional game and fish, a large species of soft-shell turtle plies the Amazon, similar to the big cooter that lives in the lakes of central Florida. These things can weigh 30 pounds or better, have a neck as long as your arm, and can strike as fast as a snake. They have a large, flat liver, which I have more than once proclaimed to be excellent eating. But I also want to point out that this simple recipe (adapted here from Marks's *The Exotic Kitchens of Peru*) can also be cooked with fresh venison liver. So, be sure to take along a pinch or two of freshly ground cumin the next time you head for camp. It makes the difference

1 pound turtle liver (or whitetail liver)
2 teaspoons salt
¼ teaspoon ground cumin
cooking oil

Slice the liver into thin pieces, about ¼ inch. Sprinkle with salt and cumin. Heat a little cooking oil in a skillet and fry the liver strips over rather low heat for 2 or 3 minutes, turning a time or two.

Serve hot, perhaps along with steamed quinoa (or rice), baked plantains, sautéed onion rings, and corn pone, topped off with tropical fruits. In camp, sautéed onions rings and mushrooms will do, perhaps cooked in the skillet along with the liver.

Newfie Cod Tongues

The heads of Atlantic cod are sometimes cut in two, sprinkled with salt and pepper, dusted with flour, and fried until golden brown on both sides. More often, the best parts of the cod heads—the cheeks and the tongues—are removed and fried separately, sometimes along with the sounds (air bladders). These parts are usually marketed separately (available in some seafood markets and on the Internet). In Newfoundland, the tongues are fried in freshly rendered pork fat and served along with the cracklings, which are called scrunchions, I understand.

16 medium cod tongues
½ pound salt pork (or more)
1½ cups flour
1 teaspoon salt
½ teaspoon black pepper

Cut the salt pork into ½-inch cubes. Fry these in a skillet until the oil is cooked out and what's left of the salt pork cubes are brown and crisp. Drain the browned pork cubes (scrunchions now), leaving the drippings in the skillet. Mix the flour, salt, and pepper in a bag. Shake the cod tongues in the seasoned flour, a few at a time, and lightly panfry, also a few at a time, until lightly browned. Serve with mashed potatoes and green peas, along with the scrunchions. Servings? Allow eight medium cod tongues per person.

For specific information regarding the anatomy of codfish I stand in debt to James R. Babb, editor of *Gray's Sporting Journal*, and to the culinary sports at Myron's Fine Food, who have a camp in Newfoundland. Further reading on the cookery of Newfoundland and Labrador can be found in the book *Fat-Back & Molasses*, edited by Ivan F. Jesperson, St. Johns. For a more historical approach, be sure to read *Cod: A Biography of the Fish that Changed the World*, by Mark Kurlansky. In the spirit of that text I point out that the director of the National Library of Iceland once wrote a treatise on the social values of eating cod heads: among other virtues, the practice teaches forbearance and, according to old Icelandic lore, increases intelligence.

A.D.'s Cricket Crisps

Most fish bait shops sell light brownish-gray crickets that fry up nicely. These can be purchased from wholesalers in bulk, or from local dealers who price them by the hundred—and at very affordable prices, I might add. Crickets are also easy to raise in large wooden boxes heated with a light bulb. In the wilds we find other species, including a black field cricket. These too are edible, along with the leaf cricket that rolls itself up in something like a sleeping bag, zippered together with silk threads.

In all cases, it's best to keep the crickets alive until the last moment, and most people do not feed them for a day or so prior to the feast in order to clean them out, so to speak. There are several commercial bait containers, usually a wire cage with a funnel mouth designed to dispense crickets, but these are not ideal for cooking purposes. If you have to catch and add them cricket by cricket, the first ones will be done before you get all of them into the pot. I prefer to use an empty Quaker Oats container, making it easy to dump the whole batch directly into the hot oil.

100 crickets
peanut oil for deep-frying
fine sea salt
parsley or watercress (optional)
Asian dipping sauce

Heat about ¾ inch of oil in a cast-iron skillet to 375°F. Dump in the crickets a few at a time and fry until they are crisp—only a minute or two. Remove the crickets from the skillet with a strainer and drain on brown bags, sprinkling them lightly with a little salt. Garnish with parsley or freshly snipped watercress.

It's best to eat these crickets with the fingers, picking up each one by the hind legs, which tend to stick straight up when fried in hot oil. Dip the cricket into a suitable dipping sauce, preferably homemade Vietnamese nuoc cham (see recipe in Chapter 6), and bite it off at the legs. If you are feeding snooty or squeamish folk, you might break off and discard the legs before serving and give each guest a round toothpick for dipping and eating the delicacies. The legs are edible, I might add, but the lower part sometimes lodges between the teeth or feels annoyingly like a tiny fishbone or hair hook stuck in the throat.

CHAPTER 8

Skillet Vegetables and Fruits

**Wild Mushroom Fritters, Skillet-Fried Corn,
Turkish Eggplant, Onion Rings,
Fried Apple Slices, Roasted Chestnuts,
and Other Skillet Eats**

On first thought, the skillet seems to be an unlikely utensil for cooking most vegetables. The pot, the stove-top Dutch oven, the steamer, or the oven-bound casserole dish would get top billing in any honest competition for the indispensable utensil, and these days even the grill would get a few votes. Still, the skillet can produce some very good eating and should be used more often even by vegans and vegetarians. In addition to cooking the vegetables, the uncovered skillet can produce a wonderful aroma for the cook to enjoy, as, for example, when browning a few chopped onions in butter. Anyhow, here are a few recipes to try.

Sautéed Chanterelles

Sliced mushrooms are delicious when sautéed in a little butter or olive oil.
These are good when served by themselves, or as a topping for steaks, pasta,
omelets, and so on. Often the pan drippings—butter and mushroom juices—are
also served. Sautéed mushrooms freeze nicely, making this a good recipe for
preserving big batches of wild mushrooms such as chanterelles, which are often
found in large numbers, or market mushrooms on half-price sale at the supermarket. Note also that mushrooms to be added to soups and stews are better
when first sautéed and then added to the main dish, along with the pan juices.

chanterelles
butter
salt and freshly ground black pepper

Cut the chanterelles across the gills into thin slices. Sauté a handful at a time in
butter on medium heat in an open cast-iron skillet, stirring as you go with a
wooden spoon and adding salt and pepper to taste. Cook until tender—usually
about 5 minutes. (Some wild mushrooms are a little tougher, however, and will
require longer simmering in a covered skillet.) Serve as needed—and find a use
for the pan drippings.

Note: Parsley, minced garlic, and so on can be added to the recipe, if these
fit the intended use of the mushrooms. For freezing, however, I prefer to stick to
the basic stuff. Other ingredients can be added after the mushrooms thaw.

Wild Mushroom Fritters

I owe Euell Gibbons, author of *Stalking the Wild Asparagus,* for this recipe. I have, however, added half a red bell pepper for color and some minced scallions to the fritter. I have also cooked it with elderberry blow. It's a versatile recipe, so suit yourself.

1 pound mushrooms, chopped

½ red bell pepper, finely chopped

½ cup scallions, finely chopped

2 chicken eggs, lightly whisked

1½ cups flour

¼ cup butter

2 teaspoons baking powder

1 teaspoon monosodium glutamate

salt and freshly ground black pepper

cooking oil for frying

In a 10-inch skillet sauté the mushrooms, bell pepper, and scallion in the butter until lightly done. Pour the mixture and the skillet juice into a bowl along with the eggs. Sift the dry ingredients together in a mixing bowl. Stir into the mushroom and egg mixture, making a batter.

Heat about $\frac{1}{16}$ inch of oil in the skillet on medium-high heat. Drop the batter by large spoonfuls into the skillet, as when making pancakes. Fry until nicely browned on the bottom, about 1½ minutes. Turn the fritters and brown the other side. Serve hot.

Onion Rings

Skillets work just fine for fried onion rings, using about ¾ inch of oil on medium-high heat. Any large onion will work, but white Vidalias are perfect. Smaller onions can be used, of course, but the large rings get more respect at the table. If you can't get the right kind of cornmeal (fine and soft, not hard and gritty), use the flour twice. Many people will have a favorite recipe for dipping the rings in a liquid batter instead of a dry coating before frying. Suit yourself, but remember that a thick batter tends to soak up lots of grease from the skillet. Note also that cooking a large batch of these rings takes some time. For feeding a crowd, a Dutch oven or deep fryer works quicker.

2 or 3 large white onions
2 cups white stone-ground cornmeal, fine
1 cup all-purpose flour
2 chicken eggs
buttermilk
peanut oil for frying
salt and freshly ground black pepper to taste
cayenne (optional)

After peeling, slice the onions ¼ inch thick, separate into rings, and place in a bowl. Cover with buttermilk and set aside for 2 or 3 hours. Then drain the rings, retaining the buttermilk.

Add a little salt, black pepper, and cayenne (if wanted) to both the flour and the cornmeal, putting each mixture into separate shallow dishes. Whisk the eggs together with ½ cup of the reserved buttermilk. Dip a few of the onion rings into the flour. Shake off excess flour and dip into the egg bath. Finally, dip into the cornmeal and shake off the excess. After putting about ⅝ inch of oil in a skillet and turning on the heat, bread the rest of the onions.

When the oil is heated to about 350°F, fry a few of the rings for 2 or 3 minutes, until golden brown, turning once with tongs. Remove to drain with tongs and fry a few more, being careful not to overload the skillet. Serve hot.

Note: These are usually eaten out of hand at the table with the rest of a meal, but also try them on burgers, po'boys, and such. Many outdoor grills have an auxiliary burner for skillet cooking, making this recipe fit right in with a cookout.

Sautéed Onions

Some modern chefs and even jackleg cooks are calling these "caramelized" onions. It's a ten-dollar vogue word for a very old recipe. In addition to being tasty as a burger topping or a side dish, the onions fill the kitchen with a wonderful aroma, especially when cooked in butter. Note that a large cast-iron skillet works best for this recipe. If you don't have a large skillet, cook it in two or three batches in an 8-incher.

2 pounds large onions
¼ cup butter
¼ cup olive oil
salt and freshly ground black pepper to taste
balsamic vinegar (if needed)

Peel the onions, cut in half lengthwise, and slice into half-rings. Heat the butter and oil in a 12-inch skillet. Add the onions, cover, and cook for 10 minutes on medium-low heat. Uncover, sprinkle with salt and pepper, and cook on medium heat for another 10 minutes, stirring from time to time with a wooden spoon. Watching carefully, cook for a few more minutes, until the onions are golden brown. If you burn them a little around the edges, fine. Just add a squirt or two of expensive balsamic vinegar and tell your guests that the onions are caramelized.

Fried Green Tomato Sandwiches

I've seen dozens of recipes for fried green tomatoes, and some are unnecessarily complicated. One book on cast-iron cooking sets forth a recipe calling for ten ingredients, including Sauce Rémoulade (which itself requires eight ingredients). The instructions tell us to core the tomatoes! In any case, here's a simple recipe for frying green tomatoes (almost mature but not yet ripe) and using them to make a sandwich. The idea for the sandwich came to me from the Busy Bee Café in DeFuniak Springs, Florida, which serves a po'boy or hoagie made with fried green tomatoes. My recipe is a little different, made with regular white sandwich bread. If you don't want to make a sandwich, fry the tomatoes and serve them separately.

2 green tomatoes
4 slices bacon
peanut oil
buttermilk
fine white cornmeal (freshly stone-ground)
mayonnaise
salt and pepper
sandwich bread

Slice the tomatoes and soak in buttermilk for an hour or so. Cook the bacon in a skillet until it is crispy. Drain and set aside.

Add enough peanut oil to the bacon drippings to measure about ½ inch. Heat on medium-high. Drain the green tomato slices, sprinkle with salt and pepper, and dredge in cornmeal, shaking off the excess. Fry the slices a few at the time until golden brown on both sides, turning once.

Smear the mayonnaise on 2 slices of sandwich bread. Top each slice with 2 pieces of bacon. Sandwich with slices of fried green tomatoes. Slice in half and serve at once. Go ahead. Take a bite right out of the middle.

Turkish Eggplant

The Turks like to fry vegetables, serving them cold or warm and, sometimes, in a sandwich. Eggplant is especially good fried, although it does soak up lots of grease. Happily, the Turks lean toward olive oil for frying and use no batter or breading on the eggplant.

2 large eggplants
olive oil
1 cup yogurt
2 cloves garlic, crushed
½ teaspoon caraway seeds
salt and pepper
fresh dill (optional garnish)

Slice the unpeeled eggplants into ½-inch rings. Salt the slices on both sides and place them side-by-side on a brown bag. Let drain for 30 minutes. Rinse the slices and dry with absorbent paper or towel.

Heat ¾ inch of olive oil in a large skillet. In a single layer, fry the eggplant slices 2 or 3 at a time until golden, turning once. Drain on brown bags.

Mix the yogurt, crushed garlic, caraway seeds, salt, and pepper in a serving bowl. Place the fried eggplant slices on a heated platter, pour the yogurt sauce over them, and garnish the sprigs of fresh dill around the outside. Serve with grilled meats or kabobs.

Fried Japanese Eggplant

There are several configurations for the eggplant fry. Regular eggplant can be cut into slices, or it can be reduced to fingers similar to french-fried potatoes. My favorite is to use the small elongated Japanese eggplant, cut into ½-inch wheels, with the skin left on. These rounds make a nice bite and don't seem as mushy as the larger slices of regular eggplant.

Japanese eggplants
chicken egg, lightly whisked
flour
bread crumbs
peanut oil
salt and pepper to taste
water

Slice the eggplants into wheels ½ inch thick. (Or, for french-fried eggplant, slice lengthwise and then cut the slices into fingers.) Soak the slices in salted cold water for an hour or so. Rinse in fresh water and drain.

Heat ½ inch of peanut oil in a large skillet. Sprinkle the eggplant with salt and pepper. Dip in flour, shake, dip in egg, roll in bread crumbs, and fry a few at a time until nicely browned. Drain on a brown bag. Serve hot.

Skillet Cabbage

Boiled cabbage is good, steamed is better, and sautéed is perfect, especially when cooking for only two or three people.

fresh cabbage
butter or bacon drippings
salt and freshly ground black pepper

Heat the butter or bacon drippings in large skillet on medium-high heat. Shred the cabbage and put a double handful into the skillet. Cook uncovered for a few minutes, stirring with a wooden spoon and sprinkling with salt and pepper. Continue cooking and stirring, cooking and stirring, uncovered, until the cabbage is done to your liking, about 20 minutes. Serve hot.

White Folk's Okra

Many people think that only young okra should be used for frying, and I agree, up to point—but freshness is more important than size. Even fully grown pods fresh off the stalk are good when fried. The real stuff is coated with fine freshly ground cornmeal and skillet-fried in hot peanut oil, but other breadings and other oils can be used. Note that no chicken egg or other goo is used. The cut okra has a mucilaginous quality that helps stick the breading. If you have a problem making the meal stick—which means that it falls to the bottom of the skillet and burns—douse the okra rounds in an egg wash and shake it in a bag of all-purpose flour.

fresh okra
peanut oil
fine white cornmeal
salt

Heat 1 inch of peanut oil to 375°F. Remove the stem ends and tips from the okra. Cut the pods into wheels, sprinkle both sides lightly with salt, and let them rest for a few minutes.

Shake the okra rounds in a bag of cornmeal. Remove them by hand, shaking off the excess meal. Fry a handful or two at a time (depending on the size of your skillet) until nicely browned and a little crispy on the outside. Do not cover the skillet while frying. Drain the fried rounds on a brown bag, spreading out to avoid overlapping, which can also make the okra limp instead of a little crunchy. If the okra doesn't have a little crust, it isn't fried just right.

East African Stuffed Okra

Okra probably originated in Africa, and the early slaves brought it to the New World. In Africa, the pods are eaten either fresh or dried—often with a combination in a single recipe. The flowers are also edible. Here's a recipe from East Africa (maybe by way of India) that calls for sautéing whole okra pods, more or less stuffed. It's an interesting variation on Southern fried okra, suitable for serving in New York or San Francisco.

a dozen or so 4-inch pods of fresh okra
¼ cup lemon juice
¼ cup peanut oil
2 teaspoons curry powder
2 teaspoons turmeric
2 cloves garlic, minced and crushed
salt and cayenne red pepper to taste

Starting at the tip, cut the pods of okra in half lengthwise, down to but not through the stem end. Hinge the pods open. Mix all the other ingredients except the peanut oil into a paste. Spread the paste onto one side of the split okra. Close the pods and press lightly to stick the sides together.

Heat the peanut oil in a skillet to about 325°F and sauté the okra pods until lightly browned. Serve hot with rice, fried fish, and a green salad, or with meats and vegetables of your choice.

Note: This recipe was adapted from Harva Hachten's very interesting book, *Best of Regional African Cooking*. Another recipe for okra, Pombo, called for the addition of chile pepper and dried shrimp or dried crayfish. If you like the strong flavor of dried shrimp, try adding a little dried shrimp paste to your stuffing for split okra. Or try your own combinations, leaving out the lemon juice. Try a little dried shrimp mixed into a tomato-based salsa.

Purslane Fries

Although generally considered a weed, purslane, which probably originated in Persia, has been cultivated for food and fodder in such places as Burma (now Myanmar) and Yemen for centuries. The early settlers brought it to America, where it was used mostly by the Indians and the French. (According to Sturtevant's *Notes on Edible Plants*, "In 1604, Champlain says the Indians along the Maine coast brought him purslane, which grows in large quantities among the Indian corn. . . .") In any case, purslane now grows wild just about everywhere in the Americas, free for the picking from southern Alaska to northern Tierra del Fuego. It can be raised from seeds in the home garden, and it is even available commercially in some markets, especially in Mexico. I have even seen store-bought purslane on a recent television cooking show or two. Ironically, some people who plant the seeds in their home gardens may be surprised to learn it's the same stuff they have been pulling up as weed for years!

Anyone interested in wild foods or adventurous eating can easily pick a mess of purslane in late summer or early autumn, a time when other such wild greens are in decline. This was nicely put by Paula Wolfert in her book *The Cooking of the Eastern Mediterranean*: "In late summer, when all wild mustards, nasturtiums, sorrels, amaranths, dandelions, and lamb's-quarters have withered, turned tough and bitter, and gone to seed, there is still one wild green left to enjoy—purslane. Its soft, thick leaves stay fresh even under the hottest sun."

Look for wild purslane along the edges of woods and fields and gardens. Once a stand is located, it's easy to pull a mess. A good plant can cover a square foot, and in heavy stands the plants will interlock. You can pull the whole plant, but you don't have to do so. The tips of the stems (which make the best eating, I think) can easily be pinched off in the field, and they will regenerate. Remember also that you don't have to pick very much purslane to have enough for a mess. It doesn't cook away as drastically as spinach, turnip tops, kale, or other greens.

The whole plant is edible, including the small flowers. The tiny seeds form on the end of the tips in small pod, and the American Indians ground them for use in breads. The thick leaves, which grow up to 2 inches long and ¾ inch wide, can be cooked separately, saving the stems for stir-fry or pickles. The tender tips can be enjoyed raw in a mixed salad, or they can be boiled or steamed like other greens. I prefer them fried, as in this recipe.

Being a little mucilaginous, purslane makes a purely excellent addition to gumbo as a substitute for okra. Also like okra, it is delicious when fried. So, pull a few tips or leaves for camp. Use your favorite recipe for fried okra, or try the following.

purslane tips or large leaves
chicken egg, lightly whisked
flour
cracker crumbs (crushed saltines)
cooking oil
salt

Rig for frying in ½ inch of oil at 350°F. Wash the purslane tips carefully and drain but do not dry completely. Sprinkle the tips with salt, then shake in a brown bag with flour. Roll them one by one first in the beaten egg and then in cracker crumbs. Fry a few at a time until golden brown, turning a time or two. Drain on a brown bag and serve hot.

Twice-Fried French Fries

It's best to use large, long baking potatoes for making french fries. Note that these are fried in two steps. The first fry can be done well ahead of serving time—even the day before.

large baking potatoes
peanut oil
salt to taste

Cut the potatoes lengthwise into strips about ⅜ inch square. I cut out any bad spots on the potato, but I leave the skin on. Suit yourself. Put the strips into a large bowl and cover them with ice water for 30 minutes or longer.

Heat 3 or 4 inches of peanut oil in a deep fryer to 325°F. Drain the potatoes and put them, a few at a time, in the hot oil. Fry for 2 minutes. Remove the potatoes and drain well on a brown bag or paper towels. (The potatoes will be pale and limp at this point.) Repeat with another batch until all the potatoes have been fried once. Let these drain well, or set aside until you are ready to resume cooking.

For the second fry, heat the oil to 375°F. Cook the french fries, uncovered, a few at a time for about 3 minutes, or until nicely browned. Remove to drain, sprinkling lightly with salt. Cook another batch, and so on until all ready. (Note that covering the potatoes during cooking or piling them high for draining will make them soft, without a crispy crust.)

Most people like a little catsup on the side for dipping their french fries, but a few will want to squirt some catsup onto the whole batch. Europeans seem to prefer mayonnaise for dipping. Suit yourself, or serve both in small dipping cups.

Note: Shoestring potatoes can be cooked the same way, but will require a shorter deep-frying time. Being only ⅛ inch thick, these are tedious to cut by hand, but a mandoline will do a swell job.

Fried Potato Rounds

These potatoes are easier to slice into rounds than they are to french-cut, making them a better choice for the camp cook. They should be between ⅛ and ¼ inch thick—or exactly ³⁄₁₆ if you have a precision slicer. I don't peel these, but suit yourself. Any good potato can be cooked by this method. Use the roundish medium size, if you have a choice, thereby saving the long ones for french fries. Note that these fried sliced potatoes require only a small amount of oil, whereas french fries work better when deep-fried.

medium raw potatoes, sliced
peanut oil for frying
salt to taste
Hungarian paprika

Heat about ¼ inch of peanut oil in a skillet to medium high. Fry a handful of sliced potatoes for a few minutes on each side, until nicely browned. (The slices should not overlap; so figure on cooking in several batches.) Spread the potatoes on a brown bag to drain, again being careful not to overlap the slices. Sprinkle with salt and Hungarian paprika. Serve hot.

Leftover Camp Potatoes, Old Irish Style

An old Irish favorite is made from leftover boiled or baked potatoes. They were simply sliced into rounds and fried pretty much as in the previous recipe. Sometimes they were served with fried onions and sprinkled with chopped parsley. The Irish also cooked potato rounds without any oil, as follows.

If you don't have cooking oil in camp, or don't want to use it, simply sprinkle the bottom of the skillet with salt. Cut the potatoes into rounds and cook them a few at a time in the dry skillet until crisp on both sides. Serve hot. In old Ireland these were called griddle potatoes and were eaten with butter.

Garden Medley in the Skillet

Here's a recipe that I adapted from the *Progressive Farmer*. Being rather frugal, I use the whole cauliflower, including part of the stem.

1 small head of cauliflower
2 medium zucchini
1 bell pepper
1 small to medium onion
2 vine-ripened tomatoes
1 large toe of garlic, peeled and crushed
¼ cup butter
2 tablespoons freshly grated Parmesan
1 teaspoon dried basil
1 teaspoon dried oregano
salt and freshly ground black pepper to taste
more freshly grated Parmesan

Separate the cauliflower into pieces. Trim the end off the inner core and slice it into wheels along with the zucchini. (I also cut a few slices off the tender part of the cauliflower leaves.) Seed the bell pepper and cut it into strips. Peel and slice the onion.

Heat the butter in a large skillet. Add the onions and slices of cauliflower core. Cook for 5 minutes, stirring as you go. Add the cauliflower pieces, zucchini, garlic, and bell pepper. Cook for a few minutes, stirring a time or two, and add the tomatoes, basil, oregano, salt, and pepper, along with 2 tablespoons of Parmesan. Cook for about a minute, tossing a time or two.

Transfer the mix to a serving dish, sprinkle with Parmesan, and serve hot. These measures should feed 6 folks, if you have plenty of good bread.

Variations: I really prefer to cut back on the zucchini simply because it is not one of my favorite vegetables. I also add other vegetables if I have them in the garden. Try diced rutabaga, for example. If fresh herbs are available, use them to taste, minced, instead of the dried basil and oregano.

A.D.'s Greasy Summer Squash

Many people like yellow squash and zucchini sliced into wheels and sautéed in butter or perhaps olive oil and cooked for only a few minutes, until tender. These are edible, but I seldom ask for seconds. Adding a little parsley or basil doesn't help much. The slices can also be deep-fried, but these aren't any better. Mixing the two together won't help. Truth is, quickly sautéed squash isn't much more than water and won't have much taste.

Cooking them for a long time, on the other hand, will reduce the bulk and concentrate the flavor. Yeah, yeah. I know that some people will say that long cooking will drive out the vitamins. Maybe it will—but you'll end up eating ten times as much squash, thereby getting more of the good stuff. Note that this method can be cooked with a skillet, but larger batches work best with a cast-iron pot or a deep "chicken fryer" skillet.

lots of crookneck yellow squash
3 strips of bacon
salt to taste

Fry a little bacon in a 12-inch cast-iron skillet until it is crisp. Drain and set aside. Cut the squash into wheels about ½ inch thick. (If the squash are young, it will not be necessary to remove the seeds. If old, cut them in half lengthwise, and remove the seeds and center pith with a spoon. Slice into half-rounds.)

Heat the bacon drippings and fill the skillet with squash. Cook, stirring from time to time, until the squash slices reduce a little. Cover and simmer for 20 minutes or so, stirring a time or two. Remove the lid, stir, and sprinkle with a little salt. Continue to cook and stir, cook and stir, until the squash slices break apart, cook down to a mush, and—careful now—turn brownish. Do not burn but push the cooking to the limit, stirring as you go with a wooden spoon. Servings? I don't know—but I can eat the whole skilletful for lunch along with the fried bacon and a little corn pone.

Please note that this is one of those recipes to which ingredients should not be added whimsically. Too much rosemary and such stuff may destroy the true flavor and essence and goodness of summer squash—which many of your guests will never have experienced before.

Easy Skillet Beans

I love really good Boston baked beans, cooked slowly for 8 hours or longer. But I can get by with ordinary canned pork and beans, helped along a little. My best advice is to use the unrefined Mexican cone sugar, called piloncillo, which is increasingly available in upscale supermarkets and by mail. (Ordinary supermarket brown sugar has been refined and molasses added to give it color and taste.) The piloncillo comes in 8-ounce cones and the cook has to shave off what is needed with a knife. If necessary, use dark brown sugar.

2 cans pork and beans (16-ounce size)
cured bacon
¾ cup lightly packed piloncillo, divided
1 medium-to-large onion, finely diced
1 teaspoon dry mustard
½ teaspoon powdered sea salt

Preheat the oven to 350°F. Fry 2 pieces of bacon until crisp in a 12-inch cast-iron skillet. Drain the bacon. Sauté the onion in the bacon drippings until brown around the edges. Set aside.

Mix the beans, ½ cup of the piloncillo, onions, crumbled bacon, sea salt, and dry mustard in a bowl, then turn out into the skillet. Cover with strips of bacon and sprinkle with the rest of the piloncillo. Bake in the center of the oven for about 30 minutes, or until the bacon is crispy on top.

Serve hot with barbecued pork and a crusty white bread, or with fried fish and hush puppies.

Refried Beans

Pinto beans are very popular in Tex-Mex cooking and in other places, such as Middle Tennessee. Usually, a big pot of beans is cooked and leftovers are something to be reckoned with. I like to use the makings (including a ham bone) in a vegetable soup—or mash them up and cook refried beans to be served with hot tamales or some such Mexican feed. Here's how:

Mash leftover beans with a fork. Shape the mess into patties. Heat some bacon drippings or other cooking oil in a skillet. Fry the patties for a few minutes on each side, turning once. Serve hot.

Skillet-Fried Corn

This delicious dish can be cooked plain, using only the corn fried in a little butter, or together with finely chopped spring onion with part of the green tops and half a diced red bell pepper. In either case, the fresh corn is shucked, silked, and cut from the cob with a sharp knife. Then the cob is scraped with the back of the knife to get more of the good stuff.

4 cups fresh corn
½ cup chopped scallions
½ cup chopped red bell pepper
¼ cup butter
2 chicken eggs, lightly whisked
salt and pepper to taste

Melt the butter in a 12-inch skillet. Add the corn, scallions, and red bell pepper. Cook on medium-high heat for 5 or 6 minutes, stirring frequently. Sprinkle with salt and pepper to taste. Stir in the chicken eggs and cook for another minute. Turn out into a serving bowl. Serve hot.

Note: If you want creamed corn, omit the scallions, bell pepper, and chicken eggs. Cook the corn for about 5 minutes, stirring from time to time. Add 1 cup of whipping cream. Cook on medium heat for about 10 minutes, stirring as you go to keep the mixture from sticking to the skillet or forming lumps. Salt and pepper to taste, stir again, and turn out into a serving bowl. Serve hot.

Elder Blow Patties

Here's a dish that I like to cook in camp when the elderberry is in bloom, forming large white umbels. The fish flakes can be made from leftovers, but it's really best to poach fresh fish for about 10 minutes, then flake the meat with a fork. Almost any good fish will work. Black bass flake nicely and are ideal. Use freshly picked elder blossoms. The cornmeal should be stone-ground from whole kernels; if this isn't available, use all flour.

2 cups fresh elder blossoms
2 cups cooked fish flakes
1 large chicken egg, whisked
½ cup fine white cornmeal
¼ cup flour
¼ cup milk
cooking oil
salt and pepper

Mix the fish flakes, milk, flour, cornmeal, eggs, elder blossoms, salt, and pepper. Heat a little oil in a skillet. Shape the mixture into patties. Carefully fry the patties on medium heat until each one is nicely browned on both sides, turning once with a spatula. Serve hot. Feeds 2 hungry campers. Increase or decrease the measures as needed.

Fried Apple Slices

I got this idea from *The Alice B. Toklas Cookbook*, which in turn got it from a lady in London. Miss Toklas, sidekick to Gertrude Stein, says the dish goes nicely with a pork roast that has been cooked in a half bottle of cider or more, basted frequently. I find that the apples also go with barbecued ribs and other feeds.

apples
bacon drippings
sugar
cinnamon

Core and slice the apples into ½-inch wheels. Heat about ¼ inch of bacon drippings in a skillet. Fry the apples until nicely colored on the bottom. Turn, sprinkle the top with sugar, and cook until the other side is nicely colored. Turn and sprinkle with sugar. Cook for half a minute, then turn and cook for another half a minute. Remove from the skillet to drain, sprinkle lightly with cinnamon, and serve warm with roast pork or other meat.

Fried Figs

Here's an old recipe that I found in *Gulf City Cook Book*, published by The Ladies of the St. Francis Street Methodist Episcopal Church, Mobile, Alabama, in 1878—perhaps the first of the American committee cookbooks! I have two nice very productive fig trees in my garden, so I was especially eager to try this recipe. I wasn't disappointed.

large ripe figs
butter
brown sugar

Peel the figs and cut them in half lengthwise. Heat some butter in a skillet. Sauté the figs a few at a time in the butter until light brown. Place on a serving platter or plate, then sprinkle lightly with brown sugar. Eat warm. Try these for breakfast, topped with a little heavy cream.

Roasted Chestnuts

I regret not having ordered a special chestnut roasting pan from a mail-order catalog I received some time ago. Still, my trusty cast-iron skillet does a pretty good job on coals from the campfire or at the hearth in my den.

To proceed, cut an X into the flat side of each chestnut. (Special chestnut knives with short, hawk-beaked blades are available, but a regular knife with a short, stout blade will do.) Heat a cast-iron skillet, completely dry, on coals from the fire or on the stove. Fill the skillet with chestnuts, but do not overcrowd. Roast in the fire for 4 or 5 minutes, shaking the skillet a few times, until the shell of the nuts browns a little and the X opens up. Remove the skillet from the heat but leave the chestnuts in it to stay warm. To eat, first peel off the shell and the inner skin.

CHAPTER 9

Skillet Breads

**Cowboy Biscuits, Yankee Cornbread,
Aztec Sunflower Bread, and
Cross Creek Crackling Bread,
with Notes on Crumb
and Flavor**

Most good chefs, North and South, will
agree that the best cornbreads are cooked in cast iron. But
that's about as far as the regional accord goes. The real culprit is the cornmeal itself. In the past few decades, most of
the white cornmeals were marketed only in parts of the South
and in Rhode Island. These are usually ground by small local
millers from whole-grain white corn by a slow stone-grinding
process. This meal does not have a long shelf life and will develop a strong, rancid taste. When fresh, however, it has a

pleasing earthy flavor and makes a bread that is not as dry and crumbly as most yellow-meal breads. Storing this whole-kernel white meal in the refrigerator or freezer at home helps extend its life, and I have even seen it in the refrigerated dairy section of small country stores.

For the most part, the yellow meals on the market have been milled by a high-speed, heat-producing process from corn robbed of the germ and its essential oils. This product has a long shelf life, but it tends to be dry, crumbly, and relatively tasteless, in my opinion. It should be used only in bread recipes that call for chicken eggs and other goo to stick the works together, not with the pure stuff consisting only of meal, water, and a little salt.

Along with a few other writers, I have argued, sometimes hotly, about the loss of good white cornmeal from the American pantry. The large millers are beginning to pay attention, and some have added a stone-ground yellow meal to their line. Well, this doesn't mean very much, unless they use the whole kernel, including the germ and its oils, in the product. The result is simply not the same as stone-ground whole-kernel white cornmeal.

There are thousands of recipes for cornbread made with yellow meal and even blue meal. Some of these are quite good, suitable for serving at the table as well as for stuffings and dressings. But what I resent is the fact that the large millers, supermarkets, recipe writers, and publishers have squeezed white meal out of the mainstream of American cookery–and pretty much out of our cookbooks. Thus, we have almost lost a very good thing. I can only hope that this modest book and a few other enlightened works will help show the way back. It is with this agenda in play that I have given more recipes in this book to white cornmeal than to yellow. If I have pushed too hard here and there, I have done so in good conscience. For a different point of view—and for forty-four cornbread recipes—see Sheila Buff's *Corn Cookery* and the Yankee Yellow Cornbread recipe below.

Of course, biscuits and other breads can also be cooked in a skillet, and some of these recipes are also included in this chapter. But it's cornbread that makes the old black skillet shine.

Hush Puppies

Almost everyone will agree that an American fish fry is simply not complete without hush puppies. Hackles begin to rise, however, as soon as the ingredients are set forth. Some purists insist that real hush puppies contain only fine cornmeal, water, and salt, all of which must be mixed into a mush of exact consistency, shaped into patties of the proper shape and size, and fried to perfection in a cast-iron skillet. I have both feet in this camp. Most cookbook and recipe writers, however, seem to have a deep-seated need to amplify instead of simplify a list of ingredients, adding all manner of stuff, including chicken eggs and chopped onion and even beer.

Some jackleg chefs and cookbook writers use the coarse yellow cornmeal, and editors allow it. I've even eaten hush puppies made from blue meal from the land of the Zuni, west of the Pecos. This stuff might be all right with those Yaqui catfish taken from the desert creeks of Arizona, but in my opinion it will ruin a mess of good Mississippi channel cats, Maine white perch, Minnesota walleye, or California grunion.

I won't get into a windy discussion, at this time, of what sort of fat or oil should be used for frying good hush puppies, but I'll have to say that bacon drippings are hard to beat for brute flavor. These days, however, many people will want to avoid animal fat altogether because it is high in cholesterol. Canola oil seems to be coming on strong these days, but I still prefer peanut oil. It has a high smoke point, it's tasteless, and it doesn't absorb much odor.

Measures? I've never seen a cook measure out the ingredients for making this kind of hush puppy or corn pone. Most of us go by the consistency of the batter. Exact measurements are not a good idea, really, because, it seems, each batch of meal is different. For starters, however, you may want to try the following:

2 level cups of fine white stone-ground cornmeal
peanut oil
1⅞ cups hot water
salt

Start by mixing white cornmeal in hot water and a little peanut oil until you have a mush that will drop nicely from a kitchen spoon, making a piece about the size of a chicken egg. Stir in a little salt, then let the mixture sit while you heat ⅞ inch of peanut oil in a cast-iron skillet. Spoon the batter into the hot peanut oil. If the mixture is just right, the batter will flatten slightly as it settles on the bottom of the skillet. Proceed until the pan is almost full of hush puppies. Cook the hush puppies on both sides over medium heat. When done, the outside of the hush puppy should be golden and crunchy, but the inside should be mushy when hot. When the pieces are done to your liking, take them up with a spatula or tongs and let them drain on a brown bag. As the they cool off a little, the inside will firm up considerably.

Remember that the above combination of ingredients is guaranteed to produce the world's best hush puppies only if you have the right cornmeal. Substitute regular supermarket meal at your culinary peril. Most ordinary dogs will eat the hush puppies, but my dog Nosher says the stuff is unfit for canine consumption.

Yet, there are thousands upon thousands of recipes for this yellow-meal bread, calling for all manner of ingredients. For example, a well-known New York literary editor by the name of Angus Cameron, co-author of the *L.L. Bean Game & Fish Cookbook*, set forth a recipe for mixing yellow cornmeal, wheat flour, baking powder, milk, and chicken egg. This mix he called "corn pone" and said that he served it in the morning along with jam and jelly. Also in the believe-it-or-not category, George Leonard Herter said that he puts ammonia bicarbonate into his hush puppies—and eats them with mayonnaise.

It seems obvious to me that some very good people all over this great country of ours have been searching desperately for the right stuff, and that they have gone far astray. Trying to satisfy a yearning, they have added all manner of extraneous ingredients to hush puppies. They are going the wrong way, however, and should return to the basics. The classic unleavened corn pone mixture as set forth above is pure and simple—if you have the right kind of meal. If you can't find a local miller, consider buying yourself a kitchen grain mill. There are several electric and hand-cranked models available in reasonable prices.

Cross Creek Crackling Bread

Many are the recipes for crackling bread, and many of these start with the wrong ingredients. If you don't know the difference between cracklings and pork skins, see the recipe in Chapter 12. This recipe has been adapted from *Cross Creek Cookery* by Marjorie Kinnan Rawlings, who said that the cracklings should be no larger than a pea. Larger cracklings, if skinless and properly made, can easily be crumbled down to size—but do not crush them too finely, for they should produce a crunch in the bread. Ms. Rawlings adds that the cracklings can turn po' folks' cornbread into a delicacy unobtainable in high places. Clearly, however, much depends on having good cracklings. And good meal—but don't get me started on that subject again.

2 cups white whole-kernel cornmeal
½ cup cracklings
½ cup skimmed milk
½ cup water
1 large chicken egg
3 teaspoons baking powder
1 teaspoon salt

Sift all the dry ingredients into a large bowl. Mix in the milk and water, stirring until smooth. Stir in the chicken egg, mixing well. Let sit while you preheat the oven to 400°F.

Stir the cracklings into the batter. Lightly grease a 12-inch skillet, pour in the batter, and bake in the center of the preheated oven for about 30 minutes. Serve hot. Like many country people back during the Great Depression, I can make a meal of this crackling bread, eaten with nothing more than thick buttermilk.

Mama's Crusty Corn Pone

My mother had a way of making hand-shaped pones with a crusty bottom and a wavy two-toned top. She didn't use a recipe, so I am proceeding cautiously. (The ingredients list looks almost identical to other cornbread recipes I have published, but the technique is different. This just goes to show that two people cooking the same recipe will be likely to come up with vastly different results.) You need, of course, finely ground whole-kernel white cornmeal and bacon drippings.

finely ground white cornmeal
bacon drippings
hot water
salt and pepper

Pour some cornmeal into a bowl and mix in some salt and pepper. Add enough hot water to make a stiff dough, mixing well. Stir in a small amount of bacon drippings. Let sit for 20 minutes or so, while the oven preheats to about 350°F. Add a little more water to the dough if needed and shape the into three hand-shaped pones, just large enough to fit into an 11- or 12-inch skillet. The pones should be about 1 inch thick.

Heat about 1/16 inch of bacon drippings in a skillet, saving a little of the bacon drippings at room temperature for later use. When it is hot, carefully add the corn pones one at a time. They should touch here and there but should not meld together. Using one hand, lightly dip the bottom of your fingers into the reserved bacon drippings. Then lightly pat the top of each pone, making a wavy surface.

Put the skillet into the oven and bake until the pones are lightly browned on top, with a few dark peaks. If all has gone well, the bread will have a crusty bottom and a tasty, attractive top. Serve as you would any other bread—or eat hot, slathered shamelessly with fresh butter.

A Yankee Cornbread

Mark Twain once wrote that Yankees don't know how to make good cornbread. They may think they know, he went on, but they really don't. I agree. Thousands of recipes these days make it hard to tell what's what, but I believe that this recipe, adapted from Sheila Buff's *Corn Cookery*, is the real stuff, for better or worse. The use of chicken egg, baking powder, milk, wheat flour, and even sugar seems to be typical.

1 cup cornmeal

1 cup flour

1 cup milk

¼ cup sugar

¼ cup butter

2 chicken eggs

1 tablespoon baking powder

½ teaspoon salt

Preheat the oven to 400°F. Place the butter in an 8-inch cast-iron skillet and put it into the oven. In a suitable bowl, mix the cornmeal, flour, baking powder, sugar, and salt. In a smaller bowl, whisk together the eggs and milk.

Using your heat-proof glove to hold the hot skillet handle, swirl the melted butter around in the skillet to coat the sides of the skillet, then pour it out of the skillet into the egg mixture. Stir this into the dry mixture and turn the batter out into the hot skillet. Bake in the center of the oven for 20 to 25 minutes, until the top is golden brown and the bread is starting to pull away from the sides of the skillet.

Cowboy Biscuits

The original Dutch oven, sitting on short legs and fitted with a flanged lid, was ideal for hearthside cooking at the early homestead. On the go, a skillet was easier to manage.

2 cups flour
¾ cup buttermilk or sour milk
¼ cup shortening or lard
cooking oil
1 teaspoon baking soda
1 teaspoon salt

Mix the flour, baking soda, and salt in a bowl. Cut in the shortening, working until the mixture has a texture similar to coarse bread crumbs. Make a hole in the mixture and pour in the buttermilk. Stir from the center outward until the dough sticks together. Do not overwork. Lightly flour a smooth surface and knead the dough 10 times.

Heat 1 inch of oil in a skillet to about 375°F. Pinch off pieces of the dough about the size of a golf ball, rolling them as you go. These will increase in size as they cook. Place the balls, a few at a time, into the hot oil. Fry for 2 minutes on each side, turning once. Drain on a brown bag and serve hot.

Note: I usually use cultured buttermilk (the kind sold in modern supermarkets) for this recipe, but dried buttermilk, mixed as directed on the package, can be used in camp. Also, sour milk can be used instead of buttermilk.

Skillet-Baked Biscuits

The best biscuits I ever ate were made during a local flood a few years ago here in Florida. My cabin on Dead Lakes was knee-deep in water and for several nights I stayed in a Red Cross shelter in the Community Center in Wewahitchka. My dog Nosher slept in the truck out front and was not allowed in the shelter. A local volunteer, a big and pleasingly plump woman, brought in some cast-iron skillets, and in these she cooked our breakfast—usually bacon, eggs, and biscuits. I don't have her recipe, but she gave all the credit to the cast-iron skillets, which she used to hold the biscuits like any other pan while they baked in the oven.

I always brought Nosher one or two of the biscuits when I came out in the morning, and she thought they were mighty fine. After two or three days the floodwaters receded, and Nosher and I returned to our cabin, with fond memories of a plump country lady who liked to cook for homeless old men and their dogs.

Since then I have seen special cast-iron biscuit cookers with circular compartments to hold the biscuits, but I think the regular round skillets work better. It's best to place five or six biscuits along the perimeter, arranged so that they touch the cast iron on the outside and touch each other lightly on two sides. The cast-iron sides and bottom will put a nice crust on the biscuits, with a soft spot where two biscuits touched. The soft spot makes it easer to split the biscuits in half with your fingers, as biscuits are almost always eaten. The soft spot is also great if the kids want to wallow out a hole with a finger and pour in some honey or molasses.

Anyhow, try your favorite cast-iron skillet instead of a pan the next time you bake biscuits. Use your grandmother's recipe, starting from scratch, or perhaps use a biscuit mix, pretty much as follows.

2¼ cups Bisquick mix
⅔ cup milk
salt to taste
bacon drippings

Preheat the oven to 450°F and warm a 12-inch cast-iron skillet. Mix the Bisquick, milk, and salt until you have a soft dough. Do not overmix. Knead dough 10 times—no more. Dust a smooth board with Bisquick or flour and roll out the dough until it is about ½ inch thick. Cut into rounds with a 2½- or 3-inch cookie wheel.

Lightly grease the bottom and sides of the warmed skillet with bacon drippings. Fit the biscuits in the skillet, putting one in the middle. Pat a small amount of bacon drippings—not much—on the top of each biscuit with your fingers. Put into the center of the oven and bake for 8 to 10 minutes, or until the biscuits are nicely browned on top. Serve hot.

Indian Fry Bread

I've seen several recipes for this bread and very similar ones billed as Squaw Bread. Since the Indians had no wheat before the Europeans arrived in America, the recipe, as usually published, is not an ancient one. I think it was developed on reservations, using the white man's provisions. Although it is often associated with the Plains Indians, it's served today at powwows and food festivals all around the country. Fry bread can be made in a deep fryer, but a 12-inch skillet works better, I think, for cooking the flat 10-inch rounds.

4 cups all-purpose flour
1 tablespoon baking powder
1½ teaspoons salt
peanut oil or sunflower oil
warm water

Sift the flour into a bowl, along with the salt and baking powder. Stir in 1½ teaspoons of peanut oil. Then mix in enough warm water to make a soft dough. Sprinkle a work surface with flour and turn out the dough. Knead it for about 5 minutes, or until you have a soft dough, dusting your hands and the work surface with flour as needed to prevent sticking. Divide the dough into 8 pieces. Using your hands, pat and stretch these into rounds about ¼ inch thick. (Do not roll these out.)

Heat about 1½ inches of peanut oil in a skillet to about 350°F. Fry the bread rounds, one at a time, for about 2 minutes on each side, turning once. Drain on paper towels or a brown bag. While the first round is frying, shape the second—and so on until all the bread has been cooked.

Serve warm. Leftovers can be warmed up in the skillet and served like toast with butter and honey.

Aztec Sunflower Bread

The American Indian made very good use of sunflower seeds, either whole or ground into a meal for breads and as a soup thickener. In addition to using available wild sunflowers, they also planted the seeds as a crop. In fact, the first cultivated plants in North America were probably sunflowers, especially in the Southwest. These days plants with very large seed heads are cultivated all around the world and are especially popular in Russia. The gardener can find a dozen varieties to grow, and the forager can still find plenty of wild sunflowers growing across the land from Canada to Mexico. Others can purchase whole seeds and ground meal from health food stores and by mail order, and, of course, snack packs of hulled seeds are sold as noshing fare. Even sunflower seed cooking oil is widely available these days.

2 cups hulled sunflower seeds
2 cups water
1 cup sunflower seed cooking oil
¼ cup very fresh stone-ground cornmeal
1 teaspoon salt

Put the seeds, water, and salt into a saucepan, bring to a boil, reduce the heat, cover tightly, and lightly simmer for an hour, stirring from time to time and adding a little more water if needed. Mash this mixture to a paste in mortar and pestle, or zap it in a modern blender or food processor. Stir in the cornmeal a little at a time, using just enough to make a dough. If the dough is too stiff, add a little more water. Heat the oil in a skillet until it's hot enough to spit back at you. Shape the dough into golf ball–sized rounds, then flatten these with your hands into small patties. Fry a few at a time, turning once, until the patties are lightly browned on both sides. Serve hot.

Seminole Pumpkin Bread

The Seminole Indians of Florida prepared a bread with puréed pumpkin mixed with flour or meal, and, I'm sure, the authentic version of old called for some coontie or perhaps live oak acorns or the fine flour extracted from cattail roots. So, experiment with this one if you're into wild foods.

I've seen several recipes, some calling for baking powder and baking soda, but I have settled here for self-rising flour. Some recipes call for spices, especially cinnamon and nutmeg, as used in many recipes for pumpkin pie. I have substituted allspice, an American spice that has a similar taste. Suit yourself.

The pumpkin can be freshly cooked and mashed, if available. If not, canned pumpkin purée will do. The Seminoles of old probably used some sort of wild bird eggs whenever available (seabird eggs were gathered commercially from Florida islands in recent years for commercial baking purposes), but a chicken egg will do. For cooking oil, the resourceful Seminole might have used pig lard or perhaps rendered bear fat or manatee blubber. These days the modern Indian is more likely to use vegetable oil.

2 cups cooked pumpkin purée
2 cups self-rising flour, plus a little more if needed
1 large chicken egg
water
salt and pepper
1 teaspoon freshly ground allspice berries
cooking oil

In a large bowl mix the pumpkin, flour, chicken egg, spices, and enough water to make a soft dough. Divide the dough into balls about 2½ inches in diameter. Work each ball with your hands, kneading and pulling, kneading and pulling, until the dough is elastic. Continue working—patting and pulling—until you have flat rounds about ¼ inch thick.

Heat about ⅛ inch of cooking oil in a skillet. Fry the bread rounds for a few minutes on each side, until golden brown and crisp.

Chapati

A number of flatbreads are made in Africa, India, and other far-flung places. These are called chapati, roti, and so on. Some are made with rice flour, millet flour, or a mixed-grain flour. Here's a basic chapati recipe from Swahili, as set forth in *Best of Regional African Cooking* by Harva Hachten. Although the ingredients list is quite simple, the technique should be practiced.

2 cups all purpose flour
1 teaspoon salt
a little oil
water

Mix the salt into the flour, then sift into a bowl. Stir in enough water to make a stiff dough and knead well. Plop the dough onto a lightly floured work surface and roll out into a thick circle. Brush with oil. Make a cut from the center of the circle to the edge. Then roll the dough into a cone. Press in both ends and form into another ball. Once again, roll out a thick circle, brush with oil, cut from the center to the edge, roll into a cone, fold in, and shape into a ball. Repeat twice more.

Divide the dough into 5 balls and roll these out into a thin circle. Heat the skillet, brush with oil, and cook each piece until golden brown on each side. Serve hot or cold.

Caribbean Cassava Bread

Here's a recipe from Haiti, similar to several such breads made in the Caribbean and parts of South America. I tested it with cassava root (yucca) purchased in a supermarket. If you are buying cassava in South America or on the islands, make sure that it is not the poisionious sort that might require special handling.

1 pound cassava root
2 tablespoons butter (or bacon drippings)
2 cloves garlic, minced
salt

Peel the cassava, then grate it with a fine mesh. Put the cassava pulp into a piece of cheesecloth. Holding it over the sink, gather the corners of the cheesecloth and twist it, squeezing out the liquid. Remove as much of the liquid as you can. Shape the cassava pulp into thin patties, sprinkle them with salt, and cook them 2 or 3 at a time (do not overlap) in a cast-iron skillet until they are nicely browned on both sides.

When all the patties have been cooked, heat a little butter in a skillet and sauté the garlic. Return the patties to the hot skillet, turn quickly, and serve hot.

Note: A similar bread is made without the garlic, oil, or even salt. Simply grate 2 pounds of cassava root, squeeze out the juice, and shape the pulp into a round cake about 5 or 6 inches in diameter and about ¾ inch thick. Cook the cake in a small skillet until it sets, turning once. This cake is sometimes moistened with a little milk and browned under a broiler, or fried in bacon drippings.

Singing Hinnie

All manner of unleavened flatbreads, such as tortillas and roti, can be cooked in a cast-iron skillet. Here's a similar bread cooked on the thick side, adapted from my work *The Whole Grain Cookbook*. I use a 10-inch skillet for this recipe, cooking one piece at a time. Use a true whole-grain wheat flour, which includes the germ of the wheat kernel.

3 cups whole-grain wheat flour

1 cup buttermilk

⅔ cup currants

¼ cup butter

¼ cup lard or shortening

1 teaspoon sugar

1 teaspoon salt

1 teaspoon cream of tartar

Heat the skillet on the stove-top until it spits back at you. Cut the butter and lard into the flour, mixing in the sugar, salt, and cream of tartar. Slowly stir in enough buttermilk to make a soft dough. Add the currants. Roll the dough out into a round to fit the skillet.

Carefully place the round into the hot skillet, listening carefully for the song to start. Turn off the television. Be quiet. Put your ear in closer. Listen. Hear that! Cook for a few minutes, until the bottom starts to brown nicely. Turn with the spatula and cook the other side. Serve hot with butter.

Camp Bannock

Here's an easy bread for cooking in camp without an oven—and with only a few ingredients. I use an 8½- or 10-inch skillet. Longer recipes for bannock call for more ingredients, such as chicken eggs and milk, and the real stuff (Scottish) was made with barley meal and oatmeal. Suit yourself.

3 cups all purpose flour
6 teaspoons baking powder
salt
water

Mix the flour, baking powder, and salt in a bowl or suitable container. Make a well in the middle and pour in a little water. Stir and pour, stir and pour until you have a nice dough. Knead the dough for several minutes. Flatten it out to a shape to fit the skillet.

Cook on a mixture of hot coals and ashes until the bottom starts to brown. Test for doneness. If necessary, remove from the heat and let cook in the skillet for a while until the center of the bread is done.

Note: If you have a suitable piece of iron at hand, such as a fire poker, heat it in the coals until red hot. Move the hot end about close over the bannock to brown the top as it cooks in the skillet. At one time, such metal rods, called salamanders, were widely used in hearthside cookery. Some modern cooks use a minature blowtorch to brown crème brûlée and such. The salamander heat tastes better, methinks.

Croutons

These are simply crispy squares of bread, used in salads and soups. Store-bought croutons are all right, but freshly made ones are better, even if they are made from stale bread. Most any loaf bread will be suitable, but I like to use thickly sliced French or Italian loaves with the crust removed.

6 slices bread cut into cubes
¼ cup olive oil or butter
salt to taste (optional)

On medium heat, cook the cubes in the oil or butter until they are nicely browned all around, turning and stirring about from time to time with a wooden spoon. I like to add a little finely ground sea salt toward the end of the cooking.

Variation: If you want garlic croutons, cook 4 to 6 peeled cloves in the oil or butter for a few minutes until the oil is flavored. Them remove the garlic and fry as usual. You can also start with garlic oil; that is, olive oil in which garlic has been steeped for several weeks.

CHAPTER 10

Breakfast in the Skillet

**Sopchoppy Pancakes, Hangtown Fry,
Easy Wild Mushroom Omelet, and
Cowboy Camp Coffee,
with Notes on How to
Scramble Chicken Eggs**

These days too many people eat cold cereal, Pop-Tarts, or store-bought doughnuts for breakfast, none of which require cooking. Even so, chicken eggs are still the mainstay of the American breakfast. Several egg grades and sizes are widely available in our supermarkets, but I really prefer eggs from yard chickens that are free to scratch in the dirt and chase insects in the grass. To me, these eggs have a brighter yolk and a better taste.

Most of the eggs eaten in this country are from chickens, but other kinds are popular in some other parts of the world. In China, duck eggs are highly regarded. I like them—especially those from a mallard. Other bird eggs include the whoppers from the ostrich and emu on down to the small ones from quail. In times past, wild bird eggs have been eaten on islands and along seacoasts, and not too many years ago some city bakeries purchased them from hunters in very large numbers.

I like to cook chicken eggs in a well-seasoned cast-iron skillet or griddle, but I would quickly recommend a nonstick Teflon skillet for tenderfoots. Since most egg dishes are best cooked on low heat, a Teflon or other nonstick skillet will do a good job and isn't as likely to stick.

In any case, here are a few recipes to try, along with some talking points for basic scrambled and fried breakfast eggs. A few breakfast recipes not requiring eggs are also included. Some breakfast staples, such as biscuits and redeye gravy, are covered in other chapters.

Scrambled Chicken Eggs

I don't offer a firm recipe for scrambled eggs, partly because the technique is far more important than nonessential ingredients like milk or cream. All you need is good fresh chicken eggs, fresh butter, and a little salt and freshly ground black pepper.

Lightly whisk the eggs in a bowl to break down and blend the whites and yolks. (Some people use a little water, milk, or cream to help break down the eggs, but these are not necessary if you have a good arm.)

Melt the butter in a skillet on low heat. Add the eggs and cook slowly, stirring slowly with a wooden spoon. As small curds begin to form, increase the stirring and decrease the heat to very low. Cook and stir until the eggs are creamy and set to your liking. (Note that high heat will produce harder scrambled eggs.) Serve hot with sea salt and freshly ground black pepper.

Most people like scrambled eggs for breakfast, along with toast and a little bacon, ham, or sausage. I confess to eating them for lunch or even dinner—and as a sandwich filling between soft white bread halves spread with mayonnaise.

Fried Chicken Eggs

The best fried eggs are cooked on low heat, preferably in a nonstick skillet. I use salted butter for frying eggs because it tastes good and works just fine on low heat. If I have cooked bacon to go with the eggs, however, I am likely to pour off the excess drippings and fry the eggs in what's left.

For sunny-side up, break the eggs directly into the skillet. Cover with a lid and cook for about 5 minutes, more or less, depending on the size of the eggs and the heat, until the whites of the eggs have set and the yolks look cooked around the edge. If you have used a nonstick skillet, tilt it carefully over the serving plate and slide the eggs out with the yolk up and intact. A good spatula will also work, being sure to slide the egg off instead of flopping it over.

For over-easy eggs, do not cover the skillet with a lid. When the whites are set, carefully slide a spatula under the egg and turn it over in the skillet. Cook for about 30 seconds. Slide it out onto the serving plate or platter with the aid of a spatula.

For hard-fried eggs, proceed as above for over-easy, but cook for 60 seconds after the turn.

Easy Wild Mushroom Omelet

Here's an omelet that doesn't require fancy skilletmanship. Note that beating the eggs a little before cooking makes a light omelet—but beating too much will make the eggs spongy and airy. (But see the note below.)

6 large chicken eggs
1 pound fresh chanterelle mushrooms, sliced
2 tablespoons butter
2 tablespoons olive oil
1 tablespoon chopped fresh herbs (optional)
salt and black pepper to taste

Beat the eggs lightly with a whisk, mixing in the salt, pepper, and chopped herbs. Melt the butter in a 12-inch nonstick skillet, add the olive oil, and heat to medium high. Sauté the mushrooms for about 5 minutes. Add the eggs and cook, without stirring or scrambling, until almost set. Fold over with the aid of a spatula and serve with bacon, toast, and other breakfast fare. Feeds from 2 to 4, depending on appetite and go-withs.

Note: There are several kinds of omelets. A classic French folded omelet, for example, is folded with two sides over the middle, usually covering a filling of some sort. Souffléed omelets are made by beating the egg whites until they are airy, then folding in the yolks before cooking. Flat omelets are usually served like pancakes, being a little too thick to be folded. A Western omelet is usually a flat one containing ham, onions, and bell peppers, all finely chopped. Most good family cookbooks will have recipes and cooking directions for several kinds of omelets. There are also many similar dishes, such as the one below.

Hangtown Fry

I've cooked several recipes for an old California Gold Rush recipe called hang-town fry. All of them were very good, if properly made, but my last version was my favorite (as is often the case). The dish should be cooked in a rather large skillet, about 11-inch. Ideally, the fried oysters should fit loosely into the skillet in one layer. Of course, much depends on the size of the oysters, with the best ones being just right to sit on a saltine. If you prepare too many for the recipe, fry them separately and serve them on the side. Although I consider this to be a hearty breakfast dish, it can also be served for lunch or dinner.

2 dozen medium oysters, freshly shucked
6 large chicken eggs
2 more large chicken eggs for the batter
6 ounces cured ham, sliced and diced (⅜-inch squares)
2 ounces salt pork, diced (⅜-inch squares)
¼ cup clarified butter (maybe more)
¼ cup milk
1 medium to large onion, grated
2 cloves garlic, mashed and minced
flour
cracker crumbs (crushed saltines)
Tabasco sauce
salt and freshly ground black pepper
parsley for garnish (optional)

Bring all the eggs to room temperature. Try out the salt pork in the skillet. When the cracklings are crisp, drain them on a brown bag and set aside. Whisk two eggs in a bowl. Shuck the oysters and shake them in a bag with a little flour. Dunk them into the beaten egg and shake in fine cracker crumbs.

Heat the butter in the skillet along with the leftover salt pork drippings. Sauté the ham for a few minutes, drain, and set aside. Fry the oysters a few at a time and drain on a brown bag, using more butter as you go if needed. When all the oysters have been fried, fit them back into the skillet without overlapping. (If you have too many, set some aside to be served separately.) Add the ham.

Lightly beat 6 chicken eggs in a bowl, adding in the milk, grated onion, and garlic. Pour the eggs into the skillet on medium heat. Cook until the eggs are set, lifting here and there to let the eggs run to the bottom. Put a drop of Tabasco sauce on each oyster, and sprinkle in a little salt and freshly ground black pepper. Then carefully fold the mixture, as when making an omelet, and transfer to a heated serving platter. Sprinkle on the cracklings and garnish with parsley sprigs.

Enjoy with hot coffee, hash browns, and sourdough biscuits. This fry will feed 2 gold miners or 6 modern San Franciscans. Anyone asking for catsup to pour onto the fry will be shot.

Eggs Ybor City

This dish calls for chorizo, a spicy pork sausage brought to the Americas from Spain. Today there are many variations in Mexico, South America, Florida, California, and other areas influenced by the early Spanish settlers. For this recipe, similar sausages can be used. I like one made from a mixture of venison and fatty shoulder of wild pigs, along with some red pepper flakes, sage, salt, and black pepper. Chorizo is often used in soups and stews, or in various other recipes.

This particular dish is from the old Spanish section of Tampa, called Ybor City, where it is still cooked and sometimes used as a fast supper dish. I like it for breakfast. If you can't get authentic Cuban bread, try either a French or Italian loaf. Note that the dish will need no salt or pepper if your sausage is spicy enough.

6 large chicken eggs
4 ounces bulk chorizo or country sausage
¼ cup cream
Cuban bread, toasted

Sauté the bulk chorizo in a medium-hot skillet for 5 or 6 minutes, until it is crumbly. (If you are using link chorizo instead of bulk, peel off the casing and chop it finely before the sauté.) Pour off most of the grease that cooks out of the sausage.

Lightly whisk the cream into the chicken eggs. Pour the mix into the skillet with the sausage. Scramble lightly, stirring for 5 or 6 minutes on medium-low heat until the eggs are set but still fluffy. Do not overcook.

Serve with toasted Cuban bread, buttered. This recipe makes a hearty breakfast for 2 good men. For lunch or supper, serve with some tomato-based salsa of your choice.

Venison Chops and Chicken Eggs

Here's a breakfast that can be made with slices of venison loin or tenderloin, or with small chops cut from the hind leg. The meat should be cut ½ inch thick. Allow three chops and three chicken eggs per person, if you are feeding hunters or other hearty eaters.

venison chops
large chicken eggs
all-purpose flour
salt and pepper to taste
cooking oil or bacon drippings

Sprinkle each chop on both sides with salt, black pepper, and flour. Beat both sides with a meat mallet or the edge of a heavy plate. Let sit for a few minutes. Then repeat the sprinkling and beating.

Heat a cast-iron skillet and wet the bottom thoroughly with cooking oil or bacon drippings. Cook the chops for 3 or 4 minutes on each side. Remove the chops to drain and add more oil or bacon drippings as needed, along with a little water. Add the chicken eggs, cover the skillet, and cook for 3 or 4 minutes. Do not turn.

Plate the eggs sunny-side up and top with the chops. Deglaze the skillet with a little more water and scrape up the grimilles with a spatula or wooden spoon. Reduce the liquid to a gravy and pour it over the eggs and venison chops. Eat with Texas-size biscuit halves. A little butter and wild grape jelly or honey will help finish off any remaining biscuits.

Fish Roe Breakfast

Any good fish roe with small berries can be used for this recipe. My favorite is from bluegill, shellcracker (redear sunfish), or similar panfish. Exact measures aren't required, but equal parts of roe to chicken egg by volume will be about right.

roe
chicken eggs
scallions
bacon
salt and pepper

Break the roe sacs and put the fish eggs into a bowl, discarding the membrane. Whisk the chicken eggs in a separate bowl. Chop the scallions, including about half of the green tops.

Fry a couple of strips of bacon in a skillet. Remove the bacon and pour off most of the grease. Sauté the onion until it is clear. Add the roe, stirring with a wooden spoon, and cook for a minute or two. Pour in the whisked chicken eggs and cook on low heat, stirring constantly, until set and nicely scrambled. Salt and pepper to taste. Serve along with camp biscuits and bacon.

Note: If you don't have fresh roe, steam or simmer a fish fillet for a few minutes, flake up the meat with a fork, and whisk into the eggs. Leftover fish can also be used.

Sopchoppy Pancakes

If you want to feed pancakes to a crowd, it's best to cook on a large rectangular griddle or at least on a flat circular griddle. A regular skillet won't hold many pancakes, and the deep sides make them difficult to turn with a spatula. Still, pancakes cook quickly and a skillet will make a stack in short order. I prefer to cook one pancake at a time in an 8-inch cast-iron skillet, but larger pans can be used.

I don't really have a recipe that I use religiously, and, I'll have to admit, I usually use a pancake mix from the supermarket. If you have a trusty recipe for pancake batter, perhaps from sourdough, use it instead of the mix. (I set forth some off-the-beaten path recipes in my work *The Whole Grain Cookbook*, including those made with teff, buckwheat, rice flour, and so on.)

Apart from the batter, a few rather small wild blueberries or huckleberries are nice in breakfast pancakes, but the larger cultivated berries are acceptable. Several kinds of wild blueberries and huckleberries grow in several sizes in the scrub lands around Sopchoppy, Florida. My title for this recipe, however, comes from the wonderful sugar cane syrup that is made in the area. I buy a gallon whenever I visit thereabouts. Some parts of the country will cry foul here and champion the use of some sort of local sorghum, or even maple syrup. Most of the latter (or at least what is sold to tourists) is far too thin for pancakes, at least to my thinking. I want a thick syrup or honey that isn't quickly sogged up. But suit yourself. It's also hard to beat the tupelo honey harvested from the river swamps of northwest Florida.

pancake batter (from a mix or your favorite recipe)
fresh blueberries or huckleberries
fresh butter
pure cane syrup or tupelo honey
butter

Mix the batter according to the directions on the package. It helps to mix the batter in a bowl with a handle and a pouring spout. Heat the skillet medium hot and coat the bottom with butter. Slowly pour a little of the batter into the skillet, or use a ladle or large spoon if you must. (Start with about ⅓ cup of batter for each pancake.) Pour steadily so that the stream is into the middle of the pancake. Cook for a minute and sprinkle on a few blueberries. When the bottom starts to set (peek by lifting up the edge with your spatula), carefully turn the pancake and cook the other side.

Put the pancakes on a serving plate or platter. When you get 3 or 4 (or whatever you deem a serving to be), put a pat of butter between each pancake and on top. Serve hot with the thick syrup or honey of your choice. Bacon or sausage and hot coffee complete the breakfast.

Hash Brown Potatoes

Frozen supermarket hash brown potatoes are partly cooked and cut into short strings so that they mat together when cooked. I like fresh hash browns much better, made with diced raw spuds. The measures below will feed two people, perhaps with a little left over for the dog. Both the onion and the diced red bell pepper can be omitted. Any kind of cooking oil can be used, but I prefer bacon drippings, especially from the bacon to be served with the hash browns.

1 pound finely diced potato
2 tablespoons minced scallions with part of green tops
1 tablespoon minced red bell pepper
salt and freshly ground black pepper
2 tablespoons bacon drippings or vegetable oil

Heat the bacon drippings in a cast-iron skillet. Add the potatoes, scallions, and red bell pepper, and cook, stirring and shaking the skillet as you go, for a few minutes. Sprinkle with salt and pepper. Spread the mix evenly and press down lightly with a spatula. Reduce the heat to low and cook for about 10 minutes, shaking the pan with one hand, and then press a time or two with the spatula in the other hand.

When the bottom is nicely browned, turn the potatoes with the aid of two spatulas—or by flipping if you feel frisky and don't have too much oil left in the skillet. Add a little more bacon drippings if needed and brown the other side. If the resulting pattie has held together, cut it into pie-shaped pieces for serving. If the pattie has torn apart, serve it as hash.

Skillet Bacon

Of the several ways to cook bacon, the jackleg will usually prefer to sauté it in a skillet simply because it's more of a hands-on approach and lets one appreciate the sizzle and the aroma. (Never mind who has to clean the stove.) A square skillet works a little better if it's large enough to hold the bacon slices without curving them, but any large skillet will do.

Heat the skillet on medium-high heat, then lay in a few slices of the bacon—but do not overcrowd, cooking in several batches if necessary. Cook for a few minutes, then turn one strip at a time with tongs. (It isn't necessary to try to flip the whole works with a spatula.) Cook for a few more minutes and turn again, considering each piece for doneness and perhaps adjusting the heat a little. Cook and turn until the bacon is as crisp as you like it. Note that some of your guests will want it crispy, others want it limp and chewy. The compleat cook will take pleasure in cooking both kinds to perfection. In either case, drain the bacon on brown bags before serving.

A good deal depends on the quality of the bacon, and on the cut. I prefer mine to be on the thick side. In fact, the best is sold in slab form so that the cook can slice it to order.

Old-time cooks used to strain their bacon drippings into a small grease pot to be used in cooking cornbread, camp potatoes, and so on. I still do this on a limited basis, but, unfortunately, many people consider any animal fat to be pure poison these days.

Cowboy Camp Coffee

Excellent coffee can be made without machines that spit and sputter and steam and drip. All you need is a pot or even a bucket (I have even used a salamander bait bucket). A large skillet is not ideal, but will do. Be warned, however, that the water should not be boiled or left on the fire for a long period of time, which turns the coffee into strong mud.

Any good brand of coffee will do. I like a New Orleans mix of half coffee beans and half chicory root, but suit yourself. Most of the cowboys of old used Arbuckle's coffee beans, which came with a stick of peppermint candy in the bag. This is not a bad idea for camp or on the road.

½ cup freshly ground coffee
1 quart water
½ cup cold water

Bring the water to a boil in a pot, bucket, or large skillet. Add the coffee grounds, remove the pot from the heat, and steep for a few minutes. (Do not bring to a boil after the coffee grounds have been added.) Gently pour in ½ cup of cold water and let stand perfectly still for a minute or two. This will cause the grounds to settle to the bottom. Pour the coffee carefully into cups, trying not to disturb the grounds. If all of the coffee will not be consumed right away, it's best to pour it off the grounds and keep it in a separate container. It can be reheated as needed.

Note: If you have eggshells, crumble one and add it to the pot or skillet during the boil. It will help settle the grounds. Other recipes include a little salt, and one practitioner recommends tapping the side of the pot or pan with a spoon or some such metallic object, apparently to help settle the grounds.

CHAPTER 11

Skillet Gravy

**Alaskan Dried Mushroom Camp Gravy,
Sopchoppy Tomato Gravy,
Nigerian Ata Sauce for Beef or Venison,
Tennessee Redeye Gravy,
and Other Soptions**

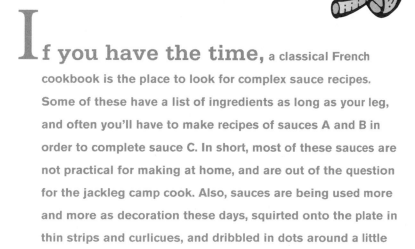

If you have the time, a classical French cookbook is the place to look for complex sauce recipes. Some of these have a list of ingredients as long as your leg, and often you'll have to make recipes of sauces A and B in order to complete sauce C. In short, most of these sauces are not practical for making at home, and are out of the question for the jackleg camp cook. Also, sauces are being used more and more as decoration these days, squirted onto the plate in thin strips and curlicues, and dribbled in dots around a little

dab of meat and a few sprigs of green stuff. Some of these composi-
tions are simply too pretty for a good man to eat.

Gravy is a less prissified concept, requiring only a few basic ingredients and not much artistic talent. Often the camp cook makes a
mess of gravy in the same skillet or pot that cooked the rabbit or
squirrel. Most country cooks over fifty years old know how to make
good gravy, and sometimes the right stuff can be found in our rural
restaurants. I remember a lunch special that I ate in The Bayou, a family eatery here in Wewahitchka, Florida, where I have lived for a few
years. They actually served up two colors of gravy on the same plate! A
white gravy topped the hamburger steak and a dark brown gravy filled
a large spoon cavity in the snow-white mashed potatoes, all flanked
with fried okra and stewed yellow squash, with a little sopping bread
on the side. In short, the plate was piled high and heaping over, leaving no room for art. It wasn't pretty. For brute flavor and a tight belly,
however, nothing in Paris can top a two-gravy country plate.

Here are a few suggestions, all made in a skillet in camp or
kitchen, along with the author's favorite BBQ soption for the patio. A
number of other sauces and gravies are made with drippings from a
meat cooked in the same skillet, such as steak au poivre. Some of
these have been covered in other chapters.

Sopchoppy Tomato Gravy

In Alabama and Middle Tennessee, a tomato gravy is really a sort of country breakfast dish. To make it, you split hot biscuits in half. Spoon stewed tomatoes, with a little salt added, over the biscuits. Pour hot cream gravy over all and enjoy. It's a very old recipe. In north Florida, however, a tomato gravy is quite different, although it is also often consumed at breakfast and is simple enough to be cooked in camp.

The version below has been adapted from Leslie Adam's recipe in *Angler Profiles*. Of this recipe, Les said, "Once you've served it on grits, you'll need no further proof of the existence of God, because only He could have created this fantastic gravy." He, Les, says the recipe originated in north Florida, and I like to place it within a 90-mile radius of Sopchoppy. In this area lies Bristol, Florida, a place of rare flora such as the torreya tree, on the banks of the Big River, as the Apalachicola is called hereabouts. Because of the unusual flora, a local doctor of scholarly bent once reckoned an area just north of Bristol to be the exact location of the original Garden of Eden.

Anyhow, for tomato gravy here's what you'll need:

1 pound smoked bacon
1 can whole chopped tomatoes (28-ounce size)
2 small cans V-8 juice (5.5-ounce size)
flour (as much as needed)
Worcestershire sauce to taste
Tabasco sauce to taste
salt and pepper to taste
grits, biscuits, or rice

Fry the bacon in a large cast-iron skillet until crisp. Remove it to drain on a brown bag. Measure (or estimate) the bacon drippings, pour them back into the skillet, heat on a medium-hot burner, and slowly stir in an equal amount of flour. Cook and stir with a wooden spoon until you have a dark brown roux (Chapter 12). Lower the heat and add the tomatoes and the liquid from the can. Add also the V-8 juice, Worcestershire sauce, Tabasco, salt, and freshly ground black pepper. Simmer for a while, stirring occasionally. Serve hot on grits or polenta, biscuit halves, or rice, with the bacon on the side.

Alaskan Dried Mushroom Camp Gravy

Dried mushrooms are even better than fresh ones for some recipes that require long, slow cooking in a liquid. They can be purchased in some supermarkets, and from gourmet shops and mail-order outfits. I prefer dried morels or chanterelles, which I dry myself whenever I happen upon a bonanza in the wild. In any case, this recipe is made in a skillet in which venison chops have been fried in a small amount of bacon drippings. It's great for camp, where, presumably, the chops would be at hand. It can also be made with beef or pork.

2 or 3 tablespoons pan drippings from chops
1 ounce dried mushrooms
1 tablespoon dried onion, minced
flour
1 cup milk
salt and freshly ground black pepper to taste
water

Put the mushrooms into a nonmetallic container, cover with water, and let soak for several hours, or overnight, turning a time or two and adding more water if needed. When it's time to cook, drain and chop the mushrooms. Save the soaking liquid.

Heat the pan drippings (adding a little cooking oil or bacon drippings if needed) and slowly add a little flour, stirring with a wooden spoon, until you have a light brown roux. Stir in the chopped mushrooms, dried onions, and a little of the soaking liquid. Cook and stir for about 10 minutes, making sure the mushrooms flavor the roux. Slowly add the milk, increase the heat, and stir briskly until the mixture boils. Salt and pepper to taste. Remove from the heat and check the texture. If it's too thick, stir in a little more of the milk or mushroom soaking liquid and reheat. Enjoy this gravy over halves of man-size sourdough biscuits.

Tennessee Redeye Gravy

This old breakfast gravy is made by first frying a large slice of country-cured ham in a skillet. This kind of ham will be quite salty, and some cooks insist on soaking the slices overnight in fresh water, perhaps changing the water a time or two. Usually, the slices are about ½ inch thick. Serve a whole slice, and its gravy, to each partaker. Dividing the measures won't work, as I found out in a small Tennessee restaurant that served country ham and gravy. One night I asked for the gravy and biscuits without the ham, but the owner rather indignantly informed me that it took a whole slice of ham to make a serving of gravy.

country ham slices
freshly brewed coffee, black and strong
freshly ground black pepper
bacon drippings

When you are ready for breakfast, fry the ham for a few minutes in a cast-iron skillet greased with a small spoonful of bacon drippings. Turn and cook the other side. Remove the ham to drain. Into the hot skillet pour a little of the coffee, stirring with a wooden spatula or wooden spoon. This is called deglazing the pan, as discussed at some length in Chapter 1. (Note that the skillet should be quite hot, causing the coffee to sizzle.) Stir in a little black pepper if wanted. If you have added a bit too much coffee, cook the gravy a little longer to reduce it, but remember that redeye is a thin gravy. Serve hot over biscuit halves, along with the country ham and eggs.

Note: One television cooking show featuring Martha Stewart omitted the coffee, using only water for deglazing the skillet. There is some confusion about how the name redeye came about, but I subscribe to an association with moonshine whiskey, which is sometimes called red-eye, and to the bloodshot eyes at a breakfast after a drunken night. A reluctant cook on the Martha Stewart show garbled the issue, saying the name came from something about not shooting until you saw the red of their eyes. Stewart knew better, I'm sure, and ought to be put in jail. Other cooks allow the use of regular supermarket ham, the kind that has been pumped up with water and chemicals. It's best to stick to the real stuff, hard and salty. Still other cooks add a little flour to thicken the gravy. Suit yourself—but don't leave out the black coffee and country ham, if you want real redeye.

Foxfire Gravy

The early settlers made extensive use of cornmeal simply because it was widely available before wheat became the dominant grain in the American kitchen. Cornmeal was sometimes called Indian meal. It's best to use fine stone-ground white meal. If you have only gritty yellow meal from the super-market, you should pass on this recipe. (See my notes on cornmeal in Chapter 9—and don't get me started on this subject again this late in the book.) In any case, I find this gravy to be a good one for camp cooking.

1 cup stone-ground white cornmeal
¼ cup bacon drippings
salt and pepper to taste
milk
water

Heat the bacon drippings in a skillet until quite hot. Mix in the cornmeal along with a little salt and pepper. Cook on medium-low heat, stirring with a wooden spoon, until the meal is nicely browned. Mix in a little water and a little milk, about half and half, stirring constantly, until the gravy is the consistency you like. Serve at breakfast over biscuit halves, or sop with corn pone.

Giblet Gravy

This gravy is traditionally made from turkey giblets for the Thanksgiving dinner, served as a topping for the dressing or stuffing. I sometimes save the giblets from chickens and game birds (even small ones like quail or snipe) to make the gravy for serving over biscuit halves. The giblets properly include the heart, liver, gizzard, and neck from the bird. Even the feet can be used, especially if you're feeding French guests. (Note that if you are dressing your own birds, the gizzard should be split open with a knife, turned, emptied of its contents, and washed thoroughly.) Hens sometimes provide immature eggs, some of which should also be used in the gravy instead of boiled eggs.

1 set turkey giblets
2 tablespoons flour
2 tablespoons bacon drippings or cooking oil
two hard-boiled chicken eggs, sliced
salt and black pepper to taste
water

Heat a little salted water in a saucepan and simmer the gizzard, heart, feet, and neck for an hour and a half, until tender. (The gizzard is especially tough.) Pull the meat off the neck (discarding the bones) and chop it along with the gizzard and heart. Discard the feet, unless you like to nibble on the toes. Put the chopped meats back into the saucepan, along with the liver. Cook for another 20 minutes or so, until the liver is tender.

While the liver cooks, heat the bacon drippings in a 10-inch skillet. Add the flour and cook, stirring as you go, until it browns nicely. Stir in about a cup of the liquid from the giblet boil. Chop the liver and add it to the gravy, along with the other giblets. Add some salt and pepper as needed. Carefully stir in the sliced boiled eggs. Serve warm in a gravy boat.

A.D.'s BBQ Soption

Shame on the jackleg cook who stays up all night slow-cooking Boston butts or shoulder to perfection—only to pour store-bought sauce over the pulled pork. It's easy to come up with your own tomato-based sauce by mixing this product and that. (Every jackleg has a secret recipe, which probably changes a little on each batch.) For flavor and texture, however, I would recommend starting with a commercial tomato-based salsa—or use your own salsa recipe. The recipe below is based on one that I came up and published in my book *Strictly Barbecue.* Use it as your own, or modify it to suit your fancy and available ingredients.

I might add that bottled salsa is now America's number one condiment, surpassing even ketchup, I understand. Hundreds of variations are available in brand-name bottles from food conglomerates on down to kitchen-table creations sold locally in Mason jars. Since most of these salsas are made with tomatoes, onions, and chile peppers, they are ideal for making an easy barbecue sauce with a Southwestern touch. Of the several such barbecue sauces that I have formulated down through the years, this one is my favorite—partly because it's also easy to make.

1 jar of medium-hot chunky salsa (16-ounce size)
1 medium onion, minced
4 cloves garlic, minced
¼ cup Mexican brown sugar (also called piloncillo, or cone
    sugar)
2 tablespoons red wine vinegar
2 tablespoons soy sauce
1 tablespoon olive oil

In a cast-iron skillet, heat the olive oil and brown the onion. Add the garlic, sugar, soy sauce, and red wine vinegar. Heat until the sugar is melted, stirring with a wooden spoon. Add the salsa. Simmer on very low heat for a few minutes, stirring constantly, until the sauce thickens to your liking. Do not burn. Excellent with pulled pork and barbecued ribs.

Note: The Mexican sugar is available in cones, which must be shaved with a knife or grated.

Nigerian Ata Sauce for Beef or Venison

This Nigerian creation is only one of hundreds of sauces made in Africa, where several sorts of hot peppers are cultivated in great plenty. I have adapted the recipe from *Best of Regional African Cooking* by Harva Hachten, but similar recipes appear in other books. In my version, I roast the red peppers over a wood or charcoal fire before proceeding simply because I like the smoky flavor; the charred skin is peeled off before using. I also increased the number of tomatoes from two to three. The ground dried shrimp used in the recipe can be purchased in some Asian markets, or can be made by pounding dried shrimp with mortar and pestle. Shrimp paste can also be used, if available. (I have also used dried salt mullet roe, grated, which makes a great seasoning.) The chile peppers can be varied according to taste and hotness. If in doubt, fresh jalapeño peppers will do.

3 red bell peppers, roasted, seeded, and peeled
3 large tomatoes, peeled and chopped
3 to 5 fresh green chile peppers, seeded and minced
1 large onion, minced
½ cup peanut oil or olive oil
1 teaspoon ground dried shrimp
salt to taste

Grind the roasted peppers, onion, green chile peppers, and tomatoes in a food mill. Heat the peanut oil in a large cast-iron skillet and sauté the ground vegetables for 5 or 6 minutes, stirring with a wooden spoon. Add the ground shrimp and a little salt. Reduce the heat to very low and simmer until the sauce starts to brown, stirring constantly to avoid burning. If needed, add a little more salt.

Serve the sauce as a topping for broiled or grilled venison backstrap cutlets, or similar cuts of beef, bison, or other good red meat. In Nigeria, the meat (often game) is sometimes simmered in a little water until tender, drained, browned quickly in very hot oil, and then cooked for a few more minutes in the sauce before serving, all of which can be accomplished in a camp skillet.

Almost Foolproof Skillet Gravy

This isn't really a recipe, and the gravy can be made in a skillet behind fried or sautéed venison chops, quail, game burgers, wild turkey fingers, and so on (see Chapters 3, 4, and 5). Simply drain off most of the cooking oil, then deglaze the skillet with a little red wine or other liquid, being sure to scrape up any dredgings that may have stuck to the bottom. (See Chapter 1 for the importance of deglazing the skillet.) Add some cream of mushroom soup, stirring until you have a nice thick gravy. Serve the gravy with the meat, or use it to top rice, mashed potatoes, or biscuit halves. I also like to use the gravy to add a little moisture to venison burgers, which tend to be on the dry side.

Excellent gravy can be made from the pan drippings from a roasted turkey or pot roast. We don't need a recipe. Just skim off some of that surface grease from the roasting pan (especially if it's a fat domestic bird), put the rest of the drippings into a cast-iron skillet on medium heat, and stir in some flour a little at a time, adding water or red wine as needed to make a gravy as thick as we want it. Stir. Taste. Stir. Taste again. Needs a twist or two of black pepper and a touch of salt. What could be easier? What better?

CHAPTER 12

Skillet Specialties

Blackened Tilapia, Big-Skillet Paella, a Few Cracklings, Skillet Jambalaya, and Other Skillet Eats, with Notes on the Shore Lunch

When framing this book in my mind, I

felt a need to put some emphasis on the relatively new culinary method of "blackening" fish and meats, made popular during the 1990s with a dish called Blackened Redfish. Since this technique is set forth incorrectly in most book and magazine recipes, I wanted to set the score right by giving it chapter status instead of merely listing it as a recipe in the fish chapter. My original plan was to have separate recipes for blackened fish, blackened venison, blackened turkey, and so on. But the technique is pretty much the same for these, so I decided to detail the method in a single recipe and list the others as footnotes.

At the same time, I realized that there are some other skillet dishes that need some emphasis for one reason or another. Three of these have to do with rice, which is quite surprising because rice is usually considered a pot dish cooked by steaming or boiling. Two of these recipes–risotto and paella–have been adapted from my work *The Whole Grain Cookbook*. The third, jambalaya, is an old Louisiana dish that is cooked in a large skillet.

After the set of rice dishes, I have added a few other skillet recipes that, I have to admit, don't fit neatly into other chapters–but who would want me to omit a method of making something as delicious as cracklings? Finally, I offer a few notes on camp cooking and the shore lunch, where the skillet is almost always in use.

Blackened Tilapia

Many recipes for blackened fish make an issue of the amount of smoke the process generates, suggesting that maybe you ought to notify the local fire department before you start cooking. There is some smoke, but proper cooking technique will hold it to a minimum, while making a perfect blackened fillet: crisp and black on the outside, moist and white on the inside. Soggy blackened fish aren't the real stuff and were probably not cooked at high heat. How high? About as hot as you can get a cast-iron skillet or griddle on an electric stove, and hotter than some briquette-burning outdoor grills and camp stoves will afford. My favorite rig for blackening is a high-BTU outdoor gas burner used to heat large pots for boiling crawfish or frying a whole turkey. Of course, you use a cast-iron skillet or flat griddle instead of a big pot. Skillets of other materials will be In danger of warping or cracking under the heat.

There are several commercial blackening spice mixes on the market. Some of these are quite hot and, if you use my method set forth below, should be diluted with mild paprika or mild powder from ancho or New Mexican chile peppers (not to be confused with commercial chili powder blends loaded with cumin).

Note that a number of recipes, some from Louisiana where the blackened redfish craze started a few decades ago, call for coating the bottom of the skillet or griddle with butter or oil before proceeding. Don't do it. That's where most of the smoke comes from. Don't worry. The fish won't stick, if it is properly coated with the spice mix and the skillet is hot enough.

The original blackened fish recipe called for redfish, as the Cajuns and Gulf Coast fishermen call the channel bass. The redfish in question had to be small simply because the fillets to be blackened must be thin. The demand soon overwhelmed the supply of small redfish, causing all manner of restrictions to be placed on the fish. Actually, any rather small fish with mild flavor can be used provided that the fillets are a little over ½ inch thick—¾ at the most. I prefer a fish with lean, white flesh. Farm-raised tilapia, sometimes marketed in my neck of the woods as Nile perch, are perfect. Fresh tilapia can be purchased in some markets, but I have taken to frozen fillets that have been vacuum-sealed in individual bags. This allows me to get out as many fillets as I need from the package without having to thaw the whole works.

If you purchase whole market tilapia, you'll have to fillet them. This isn't hard, but note that the tilapia has a row of short, odd bones on either side of the backbone, somewhat like saw teeth. The ends of these stubby bones can be cut off during the filleting process, in which case they should be removed by cutting out a thin triangular strip of meat from the fillet.

Anyhow, the spices listed below can be varied quite a lot, and some of the Cajun recipes are as long as your leg, but I do insist on having real butter (not margarine) and a cast-iron skillet or griddle.

This recipe and preamble have been adapted from a contribution I made to *One Fish, Two Fish, Crawfish, Bluefish: The Smithsonian Sustainable Seafood Cookbook*, by Carole C. Baldwin and Julie H. Mounts. Let's start with the blackening seasoning.

A.D.'s Cajun Dust

½ cup powered ancho or New Mexico chile
1 tablespoon cayenne (or to taste)
1 tablespoon finely ground black pepper
1 tablespoon finely ground white pepper
1 tablespoon finely ground sea salt
1 tablespoon onion powder

Mix all the seasonings and set aside until you are ready to cook. Note that this mix contains more mild red pepper than most recipes or commercial blackening seasonings. I use it as a sort of filler, permitting me to make a rather thick coating on the fillet as compared to a mere sprinkle. The same effect can be achieved by adding quite a bit of mild paprika or ground chile powder to a commercial blackening mix. I might add that most other recipes also call for thyme, oregano, and other spices. Suit yourself. Experiment.

The Fish

tilapia fillets
blackening dust (from above)
melted butter
a cast-iron skillet or griddle

Rig a hot fire or gas burner on the patio, or pull out some red-hot wood coals from a campfire. Heat the skillet until it is very hot. (Use a kitchen stove only if you have a good vent.) Melt the butter in a suitable container. Pour some of the blackening dust into an oblong container, a little larger than the fillets. Get ready. Dip the fillet into the melted butter to coat one side; turn to coat the other side. Shake off the excess butter, then place the fillet down on the spice mix; turn and coat the other side. Shake off the excess dust and carefully place the fillet on a platter or plate. Coat the rest of the fillets. Then look at each fillet again, starting with the first, and sprinkle on enough of the spice mix to cover any wet spots.

Now, take a deep breath and hold it. Using tongs, place a fillet onto the hot skillet. Let it sizzle for about 1½ minutes. Turn and sizzle the other side for the same length of time. (The cooking time should be varied according to the thickness of each fillet: 1¼ minutes for ½ inch thickness, 2 minutes for ¾ inch thickness.) You should now have a fillet that is dry and charred on the outside, but moist and white inside. Blacken the rest of the fillets, then serve them hot along with whatever go-withs you want.

Be warned that many of the blackening spices are quite hot, especially when used as a thick coating instead of a mere sprinkle. Many people want a glass of ice water at hand as a chaser, but it really won't help much. The heat of chile peppers comes from capsaicin, which isn't diluted by water. It's sort of like pouring water onto a grease fire, making it spread. Dairy products help tame the capsaicin in blackened fish, and I often serve a dollop or sour cream or yogurt on the side.

Note: Thin fillets from other fish can be used, along with thin slices of beef or venison loin. This is a great recipe for preparing in camp if you mix the spices at home. Most camp cooks are going to burn the fish or meat anyway, so why not do it right?

Big-Skillet Paella

This old Spanish peasant dish is best prepared with a short-grained rice called Valencia, named for the region where it is grown. The dish itself gets its name from the paella pan. This thing, about 15 inches in diameter with rather shallow slanted sides, has a D-handle on either side. It was originally designed for cooking outside over wood or charcoal and really doesn't work too well on a stove-top simply because the heat won't cover the whole pan evenly. Modern-day cooks who own such a pan use it over two eyes, turning it constantly, for the first 10 minutes of cooking, then finish the dish in the oven.

The original paella was cooked mostly with rabbits or chicken, with shellfish being added rather recently, culinarily speaking. These days, however, we see all manner of stuff in a paella, including three or four different kinds of beans and even artichokes, if you can believe that. Further, the best outdoor paella pans are surprisingly thin. This helps the expert cook to produce a tasty crust on the bottom of the dish. Paella (unlike the Italian risotto, discussed next) is a no-stir dish, thus requiring a sense of timing by the cook. Each paella pan (or large skillet) will cook a little differently, depending in part on the fire and the ingredients. If you want to try the real stuff, with crusty bottom, have at it. It would be best, however, to look for some old-time country Spanish cookbooks for more helpful instructions, if you can find them. Most of the American cookbooks and recipes will simply yield a shellfish medley cooked in rice. Some books specify "regular" rice, and I too stand guilty. In any case, here is a reasonably authentic paella, adapted from my book *Sausage*.

Although shellfish tops the dish, the essential ingredients are chicken or rabbits, rice, and chorizo sausage. Pimiento strips are traditionally used, but they are mostly for garnish. I usually use strips of red bell pepper cooked in the dish. (Fire-roasted bell peppers would be even better.) Part of the pleasure of this dish is in seeing the whole thing. So, serve it at the table right out of the skillet or paella pan, letting the diners help themselves. If you cook outdoors, you might even consider letting everybody eat right out of the paella pan, as was the old Spanish custom.

1 pound chorizo, cut into ½-inch wheels
1 chicken fryer or cottontail rabbit, cut into serving pieces
1 pound shrimp, medium to small
1 pound precooked stone crab claws
½ pound fish fillets, cut into 1-inch chunks

1 dozen fresh mussels (in the shell)

2 dozen freshly shucked oysters

3 cups uncooked Valencia rice

2 cups chopped fresh tomatoes

1½ cup chopped onion

10 cloves garlic, minced

1 red bell pepper, cut into thin strips

¾ cup olive oil

salt and freshly ground black pepper

½ teaspoon hot Spanish paprika

½ teaspoon saffron

water

Wash, trim, and steam the mussels, discarding any that do not open. Set the mussels aside, leaving them over hot water. In a separate pot for later use, bring about 2 quarts of water to a boil.

Heat the olive oil in a paella pan or large skillet on medium-high heat. Sauté the chicken or rabbit pieces, turning from time to time, until they are lightly browned. Add the chorizo slices. Cook for another 3 or 4 minutes, stirring with a wooden spoon. Place the chicken (or rabbit) and chorizo on brown paper bags to drain.

Sauté the onions in the remaining oil, stirring frequently, for 5 or 6 minutes. Add the tomatoes and turn the heat to high, cooking until much of the liquid has left the tomatoes. Add the red pepper, garlic, salt, black pepper, and paprika. Cook for a few minutes, until the peppers are tender. Add the rice and cook for 5 minutes, stirring constantly, until it starts to turn brown. Put the chicken or rabbit and chorizo pieces back into the pan. Add 4 cups of boiling water, stirring as you go. Mix the saffron into a little boiling water, then add it to the pan and mix well.

Stir in 3 more cups of boiling water. Cook for 3 or 4 minutes, then add the shrimp and fish chunks. Cook for another 3 or 4 minutes, then add the oysters. Cook for 2 or 3 more minutes, until the oysters start to curl around the edges.

Now it's decision time. If you want to gamble on a crusty bottom, cook for a few more minutes, watching the pan like a hawk and sniffing the arising vapors. At the last moment set the pan off the heat, but do not stir the paella.

Fish out some of the red pepper strips. Garnish the paella with the pepper strips, steamed mussels, and stone crab claws, set nicely into the mound. Serve immediately, along with plenty of crusty bread and red wine.

Note that this is a big recipe, suitable for feeding about 10 people, and must be cooked in a very large skillet or paella pan. It's possible to cut back on the measures. Note also that the seafood used in the recipe can easily be changed, depending on what you have at hand or what is in season. I like stone crab claws (sold precooked in most markets) as a garnish because they are so pretty, but other crab claws can be substituted. The purist may also want to use a fish or chicken stock as part of the liquid used in the dish. The bony pieces of the chicken or rabbit can be used to make a stock, as can the shrimp peelings and juice from the oysters, clams, and mussels. So . . . have fun with your paella. Remember that the real trick is to get the rice done just right without burning the bottom of the paella. If you get a crusty bottom, there's joy in that. If you burn it, well . . . curse at the author and eat off the top.

Skillet Jambalaya

To be authentic, a jambalaya must contain ham and rice. These days we see all manner of meats and seafood used instead of ham, along with all sorts of vegetables. Chicken is probably the most popular meat used, along with sausage wheels. Modern-day Cajuns who allow various ingredients will still point out that there are two basic kinds of jambalaya: brown and red. The red comes from the addition of chopped tomatoes. The brown comes in part from meat browned in a skillet (or other pan) and from the browned bits and pieces that stick to the bottom. These flavor deposits are often called grimilles in country Cajun cookery, and fond in more sophisticated circles.

In any case, I hold to the theory that the best jambalayas are cooked in a large cast-iron skillet (about 13 inches in diameter) instead of a pot, Dutch oven, or baking pan. This is especially true when cooking a brown jambalaya, as in this recipe. I insist on having some cured ham in the ingredients in addition to andouille or similar pork sausage. I also like to use the standard Creole mix of chopped onion, celery, and bell pepper.

The chicken should be cut into serving-sized pieces and boned. The bones and bony parts can be used to make a chicken stock. If necessary, however, you can used supermarket chicken breasts and store-bought chicken stock. Use plain water, if necessary.

1 pound boneless chicken cut into bite-sized chunks
1½ cups cured ham cut into bite-sized chunks
1½ cups andouille, cut into ½-inch wheels
2 ribs celery, chopped, with green tops if available
3 medium onions, chopped
2 red bell peppers, chopped
1 cup chopped scallion tops
3 cloves garlic, minced
1 cup longed grain rice
2½ cups chicken stock or water
salt and freshly ground black pepper
Tabasco sauce
flour
cooking oil or bacon drippings

Salt and pepper the chicken pieces, shake in a bag with a little flour, and fry in a large skillet with about ½ inch of oil. Drain the chicken on a brown bag. Cook and drain the ham and sausage. Set aside to drain and pour off about half the oil from the skillet.

In the remaining oil, brown the onions nicely. Add the rice and cook for several minutes, stirring with a wooden spoon. Add the peppers, scallions, celery, and garlic. Cook and stir for a few minutes, then stir in about 2 cups of the chicken stock or water. Taste, adding salt and black pepper if needed and Tabasco if wanted. Cook and stir for about 20 minutes, or until the rice is done to your liking and the liquid has been absorbed. Add more chicken stock or water if needed toward the end. The jambalaya should be moist but not soupy. Serve hot.

Note: Many recipes use shrimp or other seafood. Try these instead of the chicken, or in addition to it. Also try a small rabbit or perhaps a guinea hen, if available. Note also that many people cook jambalaya in a large covered pot, not in an open skillet. Try both ways. Some people use bone-in pieces of chicken, but eating these is a messy affair. If you start adding seafood to a skillet jambalaya, you will end up with something close to the old Spanish paella, discussed above.

Risotto alla Milanese

This creamy Italian dish is a skillet cook's dream recipe, requiring exacting hands-on cooking while at the same time allowing for a variety of ingredients and infinite variation. Risotto is best made with arborio rice, a short-grained specialty rice from Italy, or perhaps with a short-grained Valencia from Spain. Most short-grained or medium-grained rice will work—but never use long-grained.

Actually, there are hundreds of risotto recipes, all cooked pretty much the same way but with varying ingredients; in fact, risotto has become something of a fad in recent years, and whole books have been written on the subject. I consider this recipe, adapted here from my work *The Whole Grain Cookbook*, to be the classic. It calls for bone marrow, which refers to the center of large bones from beef, caribou, and other large animals, known in the far north as Eskimo butter. If your butcher can't provide the marrow bones for you, substitute more butter or margarine.

Risotto is surprisingly easy to make, If you have the right ingredients and proceed with tender loving care, making it the right dish to help the jackleg cook move up a notch or two. Use homemade chicken stock and freshly grated Parmesan instead of boxed. Don't skimp on this recipe. If you are on a diet, cook something else.

1 cup arborio rice
1 quart chicken stock
3 tablespoons butter
2 tablespoons bone marrow (or more butter)
1 medium to large onion, minced
⅓ cup dry white wine
hard Parmesan cheese, freshly grated
salt and black pepper to taste
a pinch of saffron

Put the chicken stock into a suitable pot and bring to a light boil. In a 10- to 12-inch skillet melt the bone marrow and 2 tablespoons butter. Sauté the minced onion for a few minutes. Add the rice and stir with a wooden spoon, over medium heat, for 3 to 4 minutes, until the rice turns opaque. Add the wine and cook until it evaporates, stirring constantly. Slowly add about half the boiling chicken stock and continue to cook over medium heat, stirring constantly. Do not cover. As the rice absorbs the stock, add a little more, and a little more, still stirring, until all the stock has been absorbed. This should take 20 minutes from the time the first stock was added. (When done just right, the rice will be creamy—but each kernel should retain just a hint of crunch in the center.)

Mix a pinch of saffron into the rest of the stock and stir it into the risotto. Stir in 1 tablespoon butter along with a little salt and pepper. Remove the skillet from the heat and let the risotto coast for a few minutes. Serve it hot in soup bowls, topped with a little freshly grated Parmesan. Enjoy.

Native American Stir-Fry

A true Asian stir-fry is more of a technique than a fixed recipe. The resourceful cook can usually slant the results in one way or another. I like to think of this recipe as a Native American stir-fry, helped along by a little Asian soy sauce. Like many stir-fries, it can be made in either a skillet or wok.

The ingredients call for yard-long beans. When snapped into 2-inch segments, these go nicely in a stir-fry and are increasingly available in American markets. I use them because they add a nice color to the stir-fry—and because I raise them under an old football goalpost left standing in my garden, perfect for dropping runner strings. In spite of the yard-long name, they are best when no longer than 10 or 12 inches—and when fresh. Young, tender snap beans or snow peas can be used instead.

If you are a wild foods enthusiast, try wild gingerroot instead of the Asian kind. I might point out that Jerusalem artichokes are true Native American fare, often called sun chokes, and can be gathered from the wild, purchased in modern supermarkets, ordered by the pound from seed catalogs, or raised in the home garden. Use sliced water chestnuts if you must substitute for the Jerusalem artichokes—or perhaps sliced Mexican jicama. Also try thin fingers of wild turkey breast instead of venison tenderloin wheels, or use a combination.

Note that this recipe, like most Asian dishes, contains only a small amount of meat. Increase the measures if you want more, or serve a meat or two on the side. If you don't have tender venison, use beef, pork, emu, or whatever. Just remember that the meat must be tender and should be cut into stir-fry strips. For easy openers, purchase some precut stir-fry beef at the supermarket. Use any good hot chile pepper. I prefer a smoked habañero, which is very hot.

In any case, don't let the long list of ingredients put you off. This is an easy dish to prepare, especially if you will slice all the vegetables to order shortly before time to cook. It helps to have everything ready before you heat the skillet.

½ pound venison tenderloin, cut into ¼-inch slices

2 cups cooked wild rice

1 cup sliced fresh mushrooms

1 cup sliced celery with part of green tops

1 cup sliced green onions (or wild ramps) with part of tops

1 cup sliced Jerusalem artichokes

1 cup snapped beans (young and tender)

¾ cup small carrot strips (matchstick size)

½ red bell pepper seeded and cut into thin strips

½ cup hulled sunflower seeds (salted)

¼ cup olive oil or peanut oil

3 tablespoons soy sauce

1 tablespoon sake or dry vermouth

1 tablespoon Asian sesame oil

1 tablespoon arrowroot or cornstarch

3 or 4 slices of wild gingerroot (or Asian ginger)

1 or 2 hot chile peppers (whole) to taste

salt and freshly ground black pepper

Put the meat into a nonmetallic container. Add a little of the oil and soy sauce, tossing to coat all sides. Marinate for an hour or longer.

When you are ready to cook, heat the peanut oil in a large wok or skillet. Pierce the chile peppers a few times with a fork (being careful not to lose any of the seeds), then put them into the oil, along with the gingerroot slices. Turn the heat to very low and let sit for a while—long enough to flavor the oil just the way you like it. (Taste it from time to time.) Then throw out the gingerroot and chile peppers, or tie a string around your finger to remind you to fish them out before serving the stir-fry to your guest. (I once had an important dinner guest who had to spit out a slice of ginger at the dining table!)

On high heat, add the venison to the skillet, tilting it to concentrate the oil. Stir-fry for a minute or two—no longer—and then add the sesame oil. Add the vegetables and cook for 5 minutes, stirring from time to time.

Quickly mix the cornstarch, sake, soy sauce, salt, and black pepper. (Remember that the soy sauce contains quite a bit of salt.) Add the mix to the skillet, cover, and cook for 2 or 3 minutes. Toss about to coat all the ingredients with the sauce from the bottom. Sprinkle with sunflower seeds and serve immediately with wild rice.

Clarified Butter

This butter is good for frying and sautéing on a rather high heat, which would burn regular butter. It's the milk solids that burn, and this process takes them out.

Start with a pound of unsalted butter and an 8- or 9-inch cast-iron skillet on low heat. Cut the butter into small pieces and melt in the skillet. Do not stir, but do skim off any scum that rises to the surface. Carefully remove from the heat and let the butter settle, so that the solids go to the bottom. Using a large spoon or ladle, carefully remove the clear butter from the top, putting it into a jar. Cover, refrigerate, and use as needed for frying.

Bonus for the Cook: Leave a little butter with the milk solids in the skillet and turn the heat to low. Cut a clove of garlic in half lengthwise. Put a garlic half into the skillet, cut-side down, and, using a fork, move it about under a little pressure. When hot and the milk solids start to brown, remove from the heat. Sop it up with a chewy French bread and eat it all yourself, along with a glass of wine.

Note that the ghee used in Indian cooking is similar to clarified butter, only it is cooked longer to drive off the moisture. It has a darker color and has a stronger flavor than clarified butter.

Your Perfect Dark Roux

This smooth elixir is the base for many classical Cajun and Creole dishes. It should be made in a cast-iron skillet on low heat with constant but slow stirring with a wooden spoon. If the heat is too high, the roux will likely scorch on the bottom or around the sides of the skillet, in which case your wife must throw out the whole mess and start over. Tell her to use a flame tamer if you have one, or to lift the skillet off the heat from time to time while stirring.

Use all-purpose unbleached flour and pure lard. If you don't have lard available, make your own from pork fat (see the crackling recipe below). If you must, substitute any good cooking oil or a mix, such as half bacon drippings and half peanut oil.

This recipe will take at least half an hour to prepare, but, on the plus side, it can be made ahead and stored in the refrigerator until needed for making a gumbo or some such dish. I like to use it to make a jackleg gravy in the skillet where the meat was fried.

1 cup all-purpose flour
1 cup lard

Take the telephone off the hook to make sure you won't be interrupted before you start cooking. Over low heat, melt the lard in a 12-inch cast-iron skillet. Slowly stir in the flour with a wooden spoon. Reduce the heat to very low, or use your flame tamer if available. Cook and stir, cook and stir, slowly but constantly, making sure the flour doesn't stick to the sides or bottom of the skillet. If your arm gets tired, change hands for a few stirs, but don't stop. In about 15 minutes you'll notice an aroma, indicating that you have the heat high enough. This will encourage you to complete the course.

After about 20 minutes, the roux will turn brown. Keep stirring, lifting the skillet from time to time, until the you have a walnut color with a sheen. Remove from the heat and store in the refrigerator until needed.

Note that no water has been added to the roux. In spite of what other recipes may say, do not at this time add chopped onion. Do not at this time add chopped celery. Do not at this time add chopped bell pepper. Oh, I know that these ingredients are often called the Holy Trinity of Cajun cooking, but it's best to sauté them separately and then add them to the dish being cooked. In short, a roux contains only lard and flour in equal measures. No salt. No pepper. When it's time to use the roux, a little hot water can be added to thin it, if needed.

A Few Cracklings for Old Jack Taylor

My next-door neighbor, a big man, moved to Florida after the Battle of the Bulge, saying that he never wanted to get cold again. He welcomed a change of weather in the fall of the year, however, and on first frost he always reminded me that it was hog-killing time. Jack had no hogs in late life, but he always made a batch of cracklings in an iron pot.

At other times of the year, he was content to make up a smaller batch in a skillet, using pork fat (not skin) that he purchased from a butcher. Against the advice of health-minded friends and family, most of whom feared pork fat, Jack noshed on these cracklings with his daily beer—and lived up into his nineties. But all good things must come to an end, and Jack passed on not long ago. I see him as sitting at an outdoor table on a heavenly cloud, eating cracklings and telling old tales to his old war buddies. In any case, I miss Jack—and his cracklings.

Here's his small-batch method, cooked in an outdoor shed that he built partly for cooking, complete with a two-burner stove, a refrigerator, and running water, along with shelves and cabinets to store his cast-iron pieces, pots, other gear, and a few quarts of homemade wine. For the small-batch cracklings, he selected a large, deep skillet, similar to what is now called a chicken fryer. No cover was necessary.

First, obtain a few pounds of pork fat from your butcher or from the pigs if you are butchering you own. Do not use pork skin. Put the skillet on the stove and turn the heat to medium high. Dice some of the pork, making it about ¾-inch cube. Put a handful of the cubes into the skillet to try out some lard, stirring about with a wooden spoon. Add more cubes of fat, filling the skillet to about 1 inch of the top. (Cook in several batches if necessary.)

When quite a bit of oil has been rendered, reduce the heat to medium. Do not cover. Cook and stir, cook and stir, until the cracklings have been reduced to less than half their original size and have browned nicely. Using a strainer or slotted spoon, remove the cracklings, spreading them onto brown bags to drain in a single layer. Do not cover the cracklings until they have cooled. Put another batch into the hot lard and cook them the same way. The second batch will cook quicker because of the lard in the skillet. If you have over an inch of lard, however, you might want to pour some of it out. Store the cracklings in an airtight container until needed for making crackling bread (see the Cross Creek Crackling Bread recipe in Chapter 9) or to garnish a tossed salad.

Save the lard for your wife to use for cooking fine pastries or as a general oil for skillet cookery. When cooled it will turn to a soft white mush, something like vegetable shortening. Store it in a large-mouth Mason jar in the refrigerator. Lard is hard to beat for cooking, unless you don't want the animal fat for reasons of health. There is, however, a certain joy of cooking and eating good food prepared by the old ways, and this should be factored into modern health and longevity equations, I like to think.

The Shore Lunch

A skillet is almost always used to prepare a shore lunch for anglers floating a river or fishing on a large lake. Several of the fish recipes in earlier chapters of this book work nicely for a shore lunch, but I lean toward those that require only a few ingredients—ingredients that are easy to pack and are spill-proof.

The best shore lunch cooks will of course make good use of the angler's catch or the hunter's bounty. It's also fun to make use of any edible wild foods found along the way, such as cattails (the inner stalks are sometimes called Cossack asparagus), watercress, ramps, edible mushrooms, Jerusalem artichokes, various wild nuts and berries, and so on. Any good book on foraging for wild foods will provide lots of suggestions, and we have included a few throughout in this book, such as Panfish with Fiddleheads in Chapter 6. Also, don't forget edible animals and other creatures found along the way, including crawfish, mussels, turtles, and even exotic stuff such as crickets and other bait, if you are adventurous.

To put a more sporting aspect to a fishing trip, I suggest that you take along only a slab of bacon, a little salt, and a good skillet. If you catch fish, simply sauté them in bacon drippings. If not, the bacon itself will go nicely with the acorn bread.

Most shore lunch cooks will want a skillet with a rather long handle. The short cast-iron handles get too hot and put the cook a little too close to the fire for comfort—especially while squatting on the ground to cook. Smoke is often a problem. It's almost always best to build a large fire and rake out a few coals for cooking. A keyhole design built with a few rocks is good, and shore lunch cooks often opt for cooking in the V of two small logs. In any case, it's always good to make sure you have a steady rest for the skillet, either on logs, rocks, or a rack of some sort, and have a level place to set the skillet in case you need to take it off the fire.

Although a campfire is one of the great pleasures of outdoor cookery, some people, for one reason or another, will take along gas-burning stoves to help cook the fish. Do so if you must—but be sure that the stove will get hot enough to do the job. A lot of the smaller stoves simply won't heat a large skillet hot enough to fry fish. Some of the larger butane-burning stoves, however, will provide as much heat as you need for cooking. I have used these to cook on larger boats and on the tailgate of my pickup.

The Skillet in Camp

The shore lunch comments above will usually apply equally well to camp cooking in general. Some of the best rabbit and squirrel I've ever tasted were cooked in a camp skillet. I might also point out that a successful deer hunt can provide some ready meat for camp cooking. Although some of the larger cuts are best when hung (aged) for a week or two, the ribs and tenderloins are very good when eaten right away. Also, deer liver is best when fresh the fresher the better. See the Deer Camp Venison Liver recipe in Chapter 6.

Good hunting—and good eating.

Index